ALCOHOL

How to Give It Up and Be Glad You Did

(Second Edition)

by

Philip Tate, Ph.D.

with an introduction by

Dr. Albert Ellis

See Sharp Press ◆ Tucson, Arizona ◆ 1997

Tate, Philip.
        Alcohol : how to give it up and be glad you did /
Philip Tate ; with an introduction by Dr. Albert Ellis.
- 2nd. ed. - Tucson, AZ : See Sharp Press, c1997.
        224 p. ; 22 cm
        Includes bibliographical references and index.

        1. Alcoholics - Rehabilitation. 2. Alcoholism -
Treatment. 3. Alcoholism - Psychological aspects.
4. Rational-emotive psychotherapy. 5. S.M.A.R.T. Recovery.
I. Title.

                        362.29286

ISBN 1-884365-10-8

Contents

Introduction

I am delighted to write the introduction to this revised and updated edition of Philip Tate's *Alcohol: How to Give It Up and Be Glad You Did* and to repeat the praise that I gave it in my introduction to the first edition.

For a good many years Rational Emotive Behavior Therapy (REBT) has had a specific theory of addiction and other compulsive behaviors. I described this theory in several of my early books, such as *Sex Without Guilt* (North Hollywood: Wilshire Books, 1958, 1966) and *Reason and Emotion in Psychotherapy* (Secaucus, NJ: Citadel, 1962), and I have revised it and used it with hundreds of people addicted to alcohol and other drugs and have given scores of talks and workshops on addiction for almost 40 years. Some of my findings are summarized in my books, *Rational-Emotive Therapy With Alcoholics and Substance Abusers* (with John McInerney, Raymond DiGuiseppe, and Raymond Yeager, Needham, MA: Allyn and Baker, 1988), *When AA Doesn't Work for You: Rational Steps to Quitting Alcohol* (with Emmett Velten, New York: Barricade Books, 1992), and *The Art and Science of Rational Eating* (with Michael Abrams and Lidia Dengelegi, New York: Barricade Books, 1992).

I was highly pleased when Jack Trimpey founded Rational Recovery, an alternative program to Alcoholics Anonymous, in the late 1980s, and when Self Management And Recovery Training (SMART) was founded by Philip Tate, Michler Bishop, and other practitioners of Rational Emotive Behavior Therapy (REBT) and Cognitive Behavior Therapy (CBT) in 1994. SMART is an unusual self-help organization that specifically incorporates REBT and CBT into its program for problem drinkers, compulsive overeaters, and other addicts. Organizations like Secular Organizations for Sobriety and Women for Sobriety now also offer alternative self-help programs to AA, but only SMART tries to teach its members some of the basic principles and practices of REBT.

Philip Tate, the author of *Alcohol: How to Give It Up and Be Glad You Did*, has been a highly successful rational emotive behavior therapist for a number of years, and I have been happy to supervise some of his therapy as he went through the REBT training program and qualified himself as one of our leading Associate Fellows of the Albert Ellis Institute for Rational Emotive Behavior Therapy. I have always found his work with clients to be exceptionally effective and I am highly pleased that he has become, during the last several years, one of the main SMART advisors and trainers in the United States. He has wide experience with alcohol and drug addicts and has been able to remarkably help many of them in SMART and in his own therapy practice. He has also made important contributions to the organization and procedures of SMART groups.

Alcohol: How to Give It Up and Be Glad You Did is an excellent summary of Phil's work in helping problem drinkers and other emotionally troubled people. I cannot imagine anyone who picks up this volume who will not find considerable help from reading—and, of course, *applying*—the messages in this book. Phil clearly shows how people destructively addict themselves to alcohol and other drugs and how they can use REBT and CBT to overcome their addictions. Moreover, *Alcohol: How to Give It Up and Be Glad You Did* has a great deal to say about anxiety, depression, rage, and other emotional problems that often accompany compulsive drinking and shows its readers how to precisely use REBT to minimize these problems. It thereby presents a double-barreled approach to addiction that will first help its readers stop their overindulgence in alcohol and then maintain their sobriety and other non-neurotic behavior for as long as they keep using the REBT principles and practices that Phil so lucidly explains in this exceptionally valuable book.

Albert Ellis, President
Albert Ellis Institute for Rational Emotive Behavior Therapy
45 East 65th Street, New York, NY 10021-6508
Phone: 212-535-0822; Fax: 212-249-3582
E-mail: info@rebt.org

Preface

This Book is for You

People drink and use drugs for many reasons, such as relaxation, celebration, and coping. Many discover that drug and alcohol use gives them problems, and they consider quitting. Some quit and go on to live more enjoyable lives. But many fail and continue to do badly. Why?

The beliefs they have about themselves and about quitting play an important role. Some people believe they must have the high and they can't give it up. Others believe it's too hard to quit. Still others believe they're no good, so they can't quit. Then, many label themselves as alcoholics or addicts and put themselves down for being addicted. They believe they cannot control their drinking or using, and so they continue their misery. Their thinking hooks them.

This book teaches you how to unhook yourself by changing your thinking and behavior. It presents a sensible approach to quitting based on recognizing your problem thinking and changing it. This approach is called Rational Emotive Behavior Therapy (REBT).

REBT was first developed in 1955 by psychologist Albert Ellis. It emphasizes thinking and emotions and how they effect behavior. For decades, people have used REBT to help themselves in many ways: with therapy, with self-help books such as this one, and in self-help groups such as S.M.A.R.T. Recovery (a new substance abuse program using REBT). They use it to find solutions to many problems. These include emotional disturbances, such as anger, anxiety, and depression. They use it with marital and family problems, and with behavioral problems such as procrastination and avoiding responsibilities, as well as with alcohol and other drug abuse.

How can it work with so many problems? It mostly focuses on one key element: our thinking. REBT teaches us to recognize that often our thinking is irrational and hinders effective living. It also teaches us how to recognize our irrational thinking, then eliminate it so we can live more happily and productively.

The teachings of REBT are quite different from those of Alcoholics Anonymous (AA). REBT does not label you an alcoholic or a drug addict. It does not consider you diseased, it does not teach that you are powerless to help yourself, and it does not preach a religious cure. Instead it teaches that you are a person who has problems with substance use and that you have the ability to attain knowledge and skills that can help you abstain and recover.

The different ideas inherent to these two approaches, REBT and AA, can lead to distinctly different results for many people. Craig Larsen provides a good example. He stopped drinking before going to AA. With AA, he diligently tried to help himself recover. Although he tried hard and remained abstinent, he did not succeed in many important respects. He became anxious and more depressed than he had been prior to joining AA; and he became angry with himself and disillusioned with AA.

Later, he discovered REBT. By working hard with our tools, he recovered from his AA-related problems. While maintaining his sobriety, he progressed further by overcoming his depression and low self-esteem. He discovered he was not only getting better, he was staying better. He was upsetting himself less in situations where previously he became anxious and depressed. Craig used REBT very well and he recovered nicely; many other people have done as well. Here is his story:

Craig's Story

I began drinking at age sixteen with my parents in our home. When I left home at age 21, I began buying liquor by the fifth. I don't know how much I drank, but I kept increasing. I eventually bought it by the half gallon.

I had no idea that people lived without drinking. My parents drank; my brother drank; it just didn't occur to me that you could live without drinking. I married at age 27. I didn't think drinking was a problem, but my wife did. She was not from a family of heavy drinkers. It was from her that I learned that some people live without drinking. She complained, but I kept drinking.

Eventually I was drinking all the time. I drank in the morning before going to work, and I hoped nobody would notice. (I worked as a salesman, a manufacturer's representative, and I supervised other people.) When five o'clock came . . . well, I just couldn't wait until five o'clock when I could start drinking again.

As my drinking progressed, I lost my job. I originally did not think it was because of me or my drinking, but I finally acknowledged the reality: I was taking off early to drink; I wasn't working much, and I simply wasn't functioning well enough.

After losing my job, I sold my house, and for two years my family and I traveled around the country. I didn't work and I didn't drink at all.

After the two years of travel, I took another job. I held it without drinking for another two years. Then, I took another sales position selling on the road. During one trip, I bought a bottle of wine. Within three months, I was drinking as much as ever. I was shocked at how quickly I went back to drinking so heavily my drinking was out of control.

My wife started complaining again. So I entered a brief detoxification program mainly to stop her complaining. While in this one week program, I looked around at the sad looking people going through the program and I thought, "This is where my drinking gets me, right here with the bums."

A week after leaving the program, I entered a 28-day inpatient program. I didn't accept the 12-step theory they taught, but I did learn that drinking could create problems. Most importantly I learned how I was hurting myself physically. I decided I was killing myself by drinking.

One week after leaving the treatment center, I began attending 90 meetings in 90 days with AA, combined with Adult Children of Alcoholics (ACOA). While going to these meetings, I began to believe I was a victim; I believed life had created my problems, not me. I believed I wasn't responsible for anything because I had the disease of alcoholism. I felt worse, and I was very unhappy, but I continued to try AA because it was the organization that had helped so many people.

I tried very hard to do it right, but my experience with AA resulted in my getting worse not better. I kept reading the Big Book [AA's bible, ed.]. In it, I read the promises of good results with AA. Among them was the promise I would be "happy, joyous, and free." I tried hard to work the program, but I wasn't happy. When I told the members this, they told me I wasn't "working a good program." However, they offered no further help.

They also told me it was my thinking that had resulted in my ending up at AA. I believed, "My thinking brought me to the place where I am today—an alcoholic attending AA meetings. People don't come to AA unless they have failed, and it was their thinking that got them to fail." So, I concluded that my thinking was flawed and that I could not trust my own thinking.

I continued to try, and I continued to fail. I then began to get down on myself. I was thinking, "I am an alcoholic and AA is for alcoholics. They helped millions of people yet I can't do it. I can't succeed. I am a failure."

Six months after attending AA, I began to develop anxiety attacks. I had never before had them. They occurred only during AA meetings, but I didn't see the connection between my anxiety and the meetings. I felt disillusioned and finally I stopped attending.

I then heard about the Secular Organizations for Sobriety (SOS), and I began attending their meetings. It was there that I first experienced enjoyment and happiness without drinking. I had less of a feeling of powerlessness, helplessness, and worthlessness.

Through all this, my marriage ended, and I transferred to another city. That city had no SOS groups, but it did have a group using REBT. With REBT, I began to attack my irrational thinking, and my confidence in my thinking began to return. I no longer believed I was a failure as I had thought after my experience with AA. I began to see that AA wasn't for me. I just didn't fit. With REBT, I began to learn that my thinking is important. I began to take responsibility for myself, and I began to resolve my problems.

Then I lost my job because the company I worked for went bankrupt. I began to try to cope with poverty. In reading *How to Stubbornly Refuse to Make Yourself Miserable About Anything, Yes, Anything!* by Dr. Albert Ellis, I learned that I could cope with any problem I had, no matter how bad.

One problem I worked on was the real possibility that I would have to live on the streets. I later found a job that I believed was "beneath" me. I didn't like the people I had to work with and thought I was more deserving than they were. By working on my thinking, I then concluded, "They're human, just like me." I preferred other work and the association of other people, but I no longer felt upset at the people I worked with.

Several experiences in REBT were landmark events for me:

● The first experience was using a Disputing Irrational Beliefs form (see Appendix A) in group to work on irrational beliefs. I took this form home and used it to work on numerous problems.

● Another experience occurred at a conference where Dr. Robert Dain, from Dallas, was a presenter. I had heard of Rational Emotive Behavior Therapy from Dr. Philip Tate in many meetings and I had read about Rational Emotive Behavior Therapy through the writings of Ellis. When Dr. Dain confirmed these teachings, I gained more assurance in the validity of all I had previously learned.

● A third experience occurred when I attended a presentation by Jack Trimpey, the founder of Rational Recovery where he spoke on his theory of "Recovery from Recovery." When Mr. Trimpey talked about Recovery Group Disorders (disturbances some people have in reaction to their attending 12-step meetings), he described my reaction to AA so exactly that it helped me clarify my problems and I was more able to effectively work on them.

Here are some statements that convey some of my efforts to change, what I learned, and how I changed:

- For nearly two years, I have read and studied a lot on my own. I didn't know this view [Rational Emotive Behavior Therapy] existed. I have spent a lot of time on this. I have done a lot of reading, and I have done a lot of work.

- I have learned that I am a human being. My thoughts of being human were, well, sort of like being a god. Now, I accept myself as a fallible human being.

- I studied achieving happiness as a goal. That was a whole new concept I learned with REBT, "Do what makes you happy." Before I studied REBT, I believed, "Work is the thing, and happiness is something that just happens sometimes." Now, I work toward my goal of happiness.

- I can speak more openly and honestly with people, both in recovery meetings and in the mainstream, without worrying about how they will respond.

- REBT has given me a way of examining my beliefs. It has given me a way to identify if a belief is "nutty" or sane.

- In the meetings, I feel free to communicate what I want without having to "talk the talk" in a way known only to the group.

- I can accept all parts of me. Things aren't all black and white neither my behavior nor the world; it's all a lot of grays. That's the way it is, isn't it?

- I no longer think in terms of absolutes, and I have lightened up on myself. I am doing better than ever.

Conclusion

If you are thinking of giving up alcohol (or other drugs), this book is for you. It presents many principles and techniques of Rational Emotive Behavior Therapy and applies them to problems of addiction, providing a guide for resolving self-created problems that contribute to your drinking or using.

If you are considering quitting, you can use this book to help you decide and then to follow through. Craig Larsen found help with these principles and practices. He worked hard with the information he acquired and he used it well. Fortunately, he had a choice—and so do you!

1

A Quick Start to Quitting

Some people drink heavily, recognize that they have problems with drinking, and they quit just like that. They find motivating reasons to quit, they think sensibly, and they follow through. If you can do it, then do it. However, if quitting is more complicated for you, there are a lot of things you can do. This chapter outlines many of them.

Developing Motivation

Recognize that you share with others a universal human goal: to enjoy yourself more and to suffer less. That's motivation at its best; it's a key to success, and it's certainly worth developing.

To increase your motivation, think of the gains and losses from your drinking. Write them down. Then think of the gains and losses you can expect when you quit. Write these down too. Take a close look and notice how you feel. Review what you've written again and again. This builds motivation.

Setting Your Goal: Living Without Booze or Drugs

When it becomes obvious the problems of alcohol aren't worth the benefits, set a goal for yourself: to live without booze. Then set another goal: to get involved in other activities. Commit yourself and follow through, and if you're like many others, you'll soon feel happier and will suffer less.

Because this sounds simple, it may also sound easy. Usually it isn't. Setting goals is easy; following through is not. It involves work, and people often quit working because they believe that it's too hard. It isn't. It's merely difficult, and many people follow through and succeed.

Preparing for Self-Defeating Self-Talk

Once you make a commitment, unfortunately, you can easily talk yourself out of it. You can drive by your old watering hole and tell yourself how nice it would be to have a few. You can have an argument with someone, feel angry and depressed, and then tell yourself you need a few to "settle your nerves." You say to yourself, "it's my only vice, and nobody's perfect." So you decide to drink. In each case, you think and feel before you decide to break your commitment.

Awareness of and change of this thinking is the main thrust of this book. As mentioned in the previous chapter, REBT teaches that problem thinking often precedes problem actions. Yet, often, people are unaware of their thinking. To stick to your goals, you'll do well to develop an awareness of your problem thinking so you can then more easily refuse to go along with it and, ultimately, eliminate it.

When you focus on this thinking, what do you find? Here are some examples:

- You may believe that your thinking is the unquestionable truth about reality and not subject to challenge. You may think "I need a drink" (would you die without one?); "I absolutely cannot quit" (would you quit if you were in jail for two weeks?); "There's no use in trying" (are the benefits of quitting better than the penalties of continuing?).

- Your thinking may be illogical. Example: "Because I have done some bad things, I am a rotten person." Your actions may be rotten, but you're not. You are not your actions.

- Your thinking may be selective. You may remember two or three happy events connected with drinking, and ignore ten or twelve negative things. How long has it been since you had a good, long, happy high? Be honest with yourself.

- Your thinking can take the form of rationalizations and excuses. Example, "I don't have a problem with drinking"— that, with a conviction for Driving Under the Influence and four lost jobs. Or, "Everybody has a vice, drinking is mine." If your neighbor robs banks, is it then OK for you to steal from supermarkets?

You can see that the thinking preceding your drinking isn't your best thinking. It's crooked; it's distorted; it's subtle; and it seems nearly automatic.

Some of the most damaging beliefs that distort your view of reality are those that are absolutistic and illogical. Most of this book is about such beliefs and how to change them so that you can feel better and do better. You can challenge damaging beliefs and find no evidence to support them, and you can prove them impractical. Here are some examples:

Because I like booze so much, I don't care what else happens to me.

Be honest with yourself. Of course you care. We all do. You care about your relationships with friends and family; you care about money and jobs and self-respect. I've never met a person who didn't, or couldn't, care about themselves.

I can't stand life without booze. I need the excitement it gives me.

Challenge this belief. Is it true? No. You may not like some things about life without booze, but that does not mean you cannot stand it. Like millions of people who have quit, you can stand to live without booze, and you can do well without the excitement it gives you.

It's too hard to quit and change.

Can you prove that statement? I agree it may be hard, but not *too* hard. People quit drinking every day without dying from the effort. On the contrary; they do better.

Because I've failed in the past, I'm no good, and I cannot do better.

Just try proving that one. Yes, you failed a few times. We all do. That proves that you made some mistakes—even, perhaps, a few serious ones. But it does not prove that you're no good, and it does not show anything about your ability to improve.

Overconcern about failure can be overcome by eliminating beliefs such as this one and gaining some realistic optimism. Look back; you've changed and improved many things in your life, and you can change and improve here too.

I need booze or drugs to cope with stress. Everybody has an escape and this is mine.

Prove it. Go ahead, just try. Booze does provide an escape—into blackouts and oblivion. That's a poor way to live. You don't really have to escape anything, and you'll be hard put to prove that escaping is a good thing to do! You'll do better to manage your stress, and often you'll find that you benefit from your effort.

You have just read a few of many the ideas that can sabotage your commitment to abstinence. Other chapters deal with these ideas and other self-defeating beliefs in greater detail. So now you've decided to quit drinking. What is the nature of your drinking thinking that can sabotage your goal of abstinence? It's thinking that's based on short-term pleasures, not on long-term satisfactions, and it's thinking that ignores the problems of drinking and exaggerates the benefits. It does not consider your personal health, your family, your friends, or your ability to hold down a good job. It simply urges you to go for the gusto now, and to hell with everything else.

If you have decided to quit, expect to have thoughts that will interfere with your commitment. They are against your best interest. Remember, you can have them almost without your being aware of it, so learn to recognize them quickly. Refuse to dwell on them—you know where they can lead. Get your mind and your actions on to something else.

To help you do this, try this technique: Tell yourself—out loud if it helps—that abstinence is your goal, that it's for you, and that drinking is your enemy. When you think, "Just one more," you can reject that thought because it's against you and leads to self-harm. If you think, "This time I can control my drinking," you can refuse to go along with it because, again, it's against you and leads to self-harm. Even with "I need a drink," it's clear that the thought is against your best interests and leads to self-harm.

If you've had experience with AA, you may doubt this emphasis on thinking. In AA you were told, "Your best thinking got you to here [to AA]," which means your "best thinking" resulted in drinking, and "you can't rely on your thinking." And, AA tells you not to rely on your own abilities because you have no ability to quit drinking without believing in God.

In REBT, are we saying that AA is wrong? Yes we are.

Think of it this way. The thinking that got you addicted was not your best thinking, but your worst. Learning how to quit for good is an example of your best thinking. With the use of Rational Emotive Behavior Therapy (REBT), and your own common sense, you can quickly recognize that you have the ability to change your behavior by changing your thinking.

Preparing for Feelings and Urges

After you quit drinking and start to live a normal life, you may experience what people sometimes call "cravings." That's a dramatic word for a strong urge or desire. Many people worry about them, don't understand them, and hesitate to quit because of them. Tom Horvath, a clinical psychologist and a member of S.M.A.R.T. Recovery's board of directors, lists four common misconceptions about such urges in *S.M.A.R.T. Recovery's Member's Manual:* 1) urges are excruciating or unbearable; 2) they compel you to use; 3) they will not go away until you drink or use; and, 4) they will drive you crazy.

It's nice to know these beliefs are not true. Urges are short lived, and you can help them go away. Here's how:

1. Accept your urges as a normal part of changing instead of treating them as catastrophes.

2. When you have an urge, do something—any harmless activity —to get your mind off it.

3. Gain a better understanding of your urges.

4. Look at the problems of drinking or using and the benefits of quitting.

5. Reaffirm (to yourself) your commitment to a clean and sober life.

Let's discuss each of these further. Will your urge drive you crazy? No it won't, but you can make yourself feel crazy by thinking thoughts such as, "I can't stand this; it's awful to feel this way; this is too much for me; I'm losing control of my emotions and I must be in control." Indeed, urges feel bad, but thinking this way feels worse.

Calm yourself. Frustrated desire feels bad, but it's neither awful nor too hard to bear. Consider the following: if you went on a 21-day cruise, and 100 miles out to sea you discovered that there was no booze on board, would you survive? Could you bear it? Yes, you could—and you would. Many people go through this. They have these feelings; they don't enjoy them one bit; and they survive. You can too.

So why not just challenge those false beliefs instead of fretting about them? Here are some brief challenges:

Is there any evidence that you have to give into these desires?

No there isn't. Check it out. As mentioned above, you can resist them as others have, and you can even change them. When you realize that you can stand a little discomfort, you will be back in control, and a part of your problems will be solved immediately.

Is there any evidence that you cannot stand your urges?

No! You just don't like them. If you give up the belief that you cannot stand them, part of your distress about them will go away, and you will feel better.

Is there any evidence that you must be in control of these hungers, feelings, desires or urges?

Not a bit. Check that out too. Your feelings come and go, and controlling them when you do not want them is nice, but not necessary. A key point is this: initially you may not have full control of these feelings, but you control what you do with them —you decide to act or not to act on them. That's control, and it's control that counts; and, paradoxically, if you give up this belief that you must be in control, you will gain even more control.

When you challenge your beliefs instead of automatically accepting them, you will see that your thinking isn't always accurate and helpful, and that giving up the exaggerated and absolutistic part of your thinking will diminish your emotional disturbances. By keeping the sensible part of your thinking, you will feel better and be better able to allow your urges to just come and go.

So, with your urges, challenge the thinking that leads you to do poorly. By doing so, you may see that you can tolerate these feelings, and that they will go away when you do not give in and when you switch your mind onto something else.

Another technique that can help, as mentioned before, is going over the costs and benefits of drinking (or drugging). Think of the down side of addiction. Think of the benefits of clean and sober living. Write these down. Read what you've written again and again.

Distraction, as briefly mentioned before, is another way of dealing with urges. Getting your mind off your urges and onto something else may help, whereas paying attention to them makes it easy to feel miserable and to give in when you feel an urge. You can distract yourself by engaging in activities such as physical exercise, reading a book, and talking to a friend on the phone. If you only think of something else, that will help too, but for most people that's harder and less effective. So do something and think of what you are doing.

To help distract yourself, you may practice a form of "thought stopping." Here is an example. When you are having an urge to drink or use, shout (silently) to yourself, "Stop! Get on to something else! Now!" Then follow through.

When you decide beforehand on some distraction technique, thought stopping works even better. List the many things you can do when an urge comes, such as reading, going to a movie, cleaning up your room, or working on a hobby. Go ahead, list five or ten things you can do or want to do to get your mind off the urge. Then, when an urge comes, shout "Stop!" to yourself and immediately start doing something you've planned to do.

Prepare for Lapse (A Failure)

AA lore correctly states that abstinence may be easy for the first 30 days, or even 90, when you're all aglow with your success, but then—you go out on a bender. Yes, sobriety is wonderful for a while, but often it doesn't last. To have a drink, or even to get drunk, is a lapse, a mistake in judgment, and usually it's not a major catastrophe.

A relapse is when you get back to your old drinking patterns with the same attitudes and behavior patterns. If you relapse, you've caved in—thrown in the towel.

With either a lapse or relapse, you are fully capable of recovering; it's just harder to recover from a relapse. Simply treat either as a mistake and keep working the methods that have helped.

Going From Here

If you can quit through using the information provided so far, great. Keep it up. Still, some people need more help, and more help follows in the next chapters. In them you will find information on how to handle abstinence, lapse, relapse, and recovery. Topics include: 1) how to recognize problems with drinking or using; 2) getting yourself motivated; and 3) recognizing and eliminating drinking (using) thinking, and feelings of hopelessness, low self-esteem, anxiety, guilt, low frustration tolerance, and anger.

In the latter part of this book, you will find a chapter on happiness and how to achieve it. Real recovery means more than getting sober and clean; it means regaining some or all of the happiness you sacrificed by abusing alcohol or other drugs. Finally, you will discover how to get help in a recovery program, through a therapist, or both.

2

Acknowledging Problems Related To Drinking

The first step in dealing with heavy drinking is to look at the problems it may create. People who continue drinking often recognize these problems, damn themselves for creating them, and drink to escape their misery, thereby adding to their misery. They often rationalize these problems or deny they have them, just to live with it all, and they keep drinking.

What a mess!

Instead of cluttering your mind with the nonsense of excuses and self-damnations, it's better to keep things simple. If you ever think that drinking (using) gives you problems, it does! Face it. Then take the next step and do something about it. This may not be simple, but it's our goal: to first acknowledge problems and then to change them.

This chapter lists many common problems created by drinking or using in order to help you develop awareness of them. As you read, you may recognize some problems that you haven't fully admitted. If so, acknowledge them—they are important: your awareness of them may help you quit.

Once you acknowledge that, "yes, I do have problems related to drinking," you may feel motivated to change—and that is good. I said *may* feel motivated because you may do something else when you acknowledge a problem: you may think irrationally and tell yourself that you can't stand to think about these problems, and you're no good for creating them, or worse, you may even tell yourself that these problems are not problems at all. When you do that, you may go no further in helping yourself, and you can get worse because of your denial.

To help you deal with these self-sabotaging ideas, this chapter contains suggestions and techniques to deal with them. Later, in other chapters, we present many more helpful suggestions. But for now, let's face the music. Let's look at some consequences of drinking that you may have and that you do not like.

What Is a Problem?

A problem is an unwanted event or encounter. What is a problem with drinking? It's an unwanted consequence of drinking. For instance, if you wreck your car, you have a problem; most people would agree. If you wreck your car due to intoxication, that too is a problem: one with drinking. You may not agree, saying, "That's what you expect from a drunk. Why would you consider it to be a problem?" The answer? Because you do not want it. And when you do not want something to happen—and it does—it's a problem.

Jack provides a good illustration of a person who had difficulty recognizing the unwanted consequences of his drinking. He was a client of mine who had been sober for quite some time. However, his wife was considering divorcing him because of all the hardships they had in the past (mostly created by his drinking), which included two arrests for drunken driving. During one of his therapy sessions he casually stated, "You know, my friends keep telling me that drinking gives me most of my problems, but I don't see it."

This was my reply: "When you married, your intention was not to have your wife leave you, but she wants to, mostly because of the consequences of your drinking. If you didn't drink, your marriage might not be in crisis right now. And when you drove while you were drunk, it was not your intention to be arrested, but you were arrested—two times, in fact—for driving under the influence. If you had been sober while driving, this would not have happened—right?"

Jack replied, "Well, when you put it that way, I guess I can see how my drinking gave me these problems."

Joe provides another good example. He was an Orlando S.M.A.R.T. Recovery group member (formerly Rational Recovery –Orlando). During one of our meetings he mentioned that he recently was denied a promotion. To get the promotion, he had to pass a security clearance, but he had too many DUIs on his record to qualify—three pages full! When he presented his resume with the attachment pages of his arrests, his employer simply shook his head and said, "Forget it, Joe." Joe said to us: "I had no idea my record was such a problem."

Neither Jack nor Joe could recognize the seriousness of the consequences of their drinking until they were directly confronted by it. It's an important milestone. Once you admit that drinking does create hassles for you, then you may work at fully acknowledging them and you can seriously think about quitting.

Acknowledge Your Mistakes—Feel Sorrow or Regret

You'll be wise to acknowledge mistakes because they have bad consequences and because you'll probably repeat them if you don't. The primary reasons people do not acknowledge mistakes is that they put themselves down and feel worthless when they do acknowledge them, and that they often upset themselves about the difficulties of changing. In order to avoid these feelings, they simply don't admit their mistakes; instead, they deny them or make excuses for them.

Here's an example: Let's say that your doctor just told you that alcohol is seriously hurting your health and that you would do well to quit.

The following irrational thinking and excuses might prevent you from facing this:

Irrational thinking: It's *too hard* to quit; I *can't stand* to live without alcohol—it would be *awful* to have to quit.

Excuse for Continued Drinking: My doctor does not know what he is talking about, and I will prove him wrong.

Irrational thinking: I shouldn't make mistakes; I'm no good for doing this to myself.

Rationalization for Continued Drinking: Oh, well—maybe living a long life isn't such a good idea after all.

Dispute Your Irrational Beliefs

What happens if you continue to think irrationally? You do not change—you continue the behavior patterns that created your problems and you continue to suffer the unwanted consequences of drinking.

Instead, when you notice the bad results of your drinking, work at refusing to upset yourself. Challenge your irrational beliefs and get rid of them. Here are examples:

Disputing Question: Is there any evidence that it's too hard to quit? Can I prove it?

Answer: I can't find any evidence. I can't prove it! Quitting will take effort, but not too much effort.

Disputing Question: Where is the evidence that I'm no good for doing this to myself?

Answer: There is none! I have done badly by doing this to myself, but doing badly doesn't make me bad.

Disputing Question: Prove that it would be awful to quit.

Answer: I can't! Quitting would be difficult, which I do not like. But, it's not *awful*.

Disputing Question: Prove that I can't live without alcohol!

Answer: I can't prove it! I have lived without it in the past, so of course I can live without it now.

After you eliminate your irrational thinking, you are left with the consequences of your mistake, with your thoughts about the mistake, and with a feeling of sorrow or regret—which is good. You have now taken your first step in eliminating some of the nonsense that prevents you from admitting the problem and that gives you misery. Next, you can contemplate what to do about your problems.

What kind of rational thinking would help you if you were confronted by your doctor in a real situation? You could think, "This is serious—I don't want to die; I want to live. I will do what the doctor suggests, so I can enjoy better health and a longer life." When you think this, or something similar, you can feel better and do better when facing your problems.

The brief discussion we've just had about typical upsets about problems may not be enough to help you look at your problems without becoming disturbed. This book contains much more help with this. As you continue reading about our approach and begin using it, you will probably find it more and more helpful.

Problems Created by Heavy or Addictive Drinking

In the next few pages you will find several different discussions on and lists of complications related to heavy drinking (using). Read through them to recognize those you may have now or may have in the future. As previously noted, you'll be wise to look at your problems squarely, feel appropriately bad, and then work to change them. Yes, you will have feelings when you notice your mistakes; they help you to get motivated, especially when you do so without damning yourself or putting yourself down in any way. Here are some of the serious results that may occur with heavy drinking:

Health Problems: Alcoholic hepatitis, cirrhosis of the liver, duodenal ulcers, fatty liver, gastric ulcers, gastritis, pancreatitis, neuritis, delirium tremens, hypertension, heart disease, varicose veins, and cancer of the esophagus.

Emotional Problems: Failure to deal with emotional problems except by using substances to cope (using substances doesn't "solve" problems). Self hatred for drinking or failing to quit. Exaggeration of the feelings created by depriving yourself of the drug (such as, "It's too hard to quit," and "I can't stand doing without it"). Diminished awareness of long-term happiness. Depression created by substances such as alcohol and cocaine.

Physical Dangers: Accidents and death.

Legal Problems: Arrests, court appearances, and required enrollment in educational programs (to learn about the effects of drinking).

Money Problems: Less available money due to absence from work and bills for medical and legal fees.

Shortened Life: Earlier death due to alcohol-related illnesses and accidents.

Poorer Sex: Increased probability of impotence for men and weaker orgasms for women.

Mental Dullness: Poor concentration and attention. (Many people notice improved mental functioning after they quit drinking.)

Sleep Problems: May create poor sleep. (After you have stopped drinking, you may find it hard to sleep for a while, but later your sleeping will probably improve.)

Marital Problems: Neglect of your marriage. Complaints from your spouse about your drinking. Staying in a problem marriage that you would leave if you weren't drinking.

Low Energy: Low interest in living and little desire for self-enjoyment.

Distraction from Responsibilities: Focus on drinking instead of responsibilities to family, self, and job.

Social Withdrawal: May not socialize much with people who are sober.

The following are based on the criteria for diagnosing alcohol and drug dependence from The American Psychiatric Association *Diagnostics and Statistical Manual of Mental Disorders, Fourth Edition.* Many professionals use a similar list to help in their diagnoses. Read these statements carefully to determine if you have any of these problems:

- *I often take substances in larger amounts or over a longer period than I intended.*

- *I have a persistent desire to cut down or to control my use of substances, or I have made one or more unsuccessful attempts to do so.*

- *I spend a great deal of time in activities necessary to get alcohol or drugs or in recovering from its effects.*

- *I am frequently intoxicated or experiencing withdrawal symptoms when expected to fulfill major responsibilities at work, school, or home.* Examples: *I do not go to work because I'm hung over; I go to school or work "high"; I am frequently intoxicated while taking care of my children. Or, I frequently use substances when doing physically hazardous activities such as driving.*

- *I have given up important social, occupational, or recreational activities or reduced them because of substance use.*

- *I have continued to use substances although I know I'm having persistent or recurrent social, psychological, or physical problems caused or exacerbated by the use of the substance (e.g., I keep using alcohol despite family arguments about it; I have a cocaine-induced depression; or I have an ulcer made worse by drinking).*

- *I have found that I need a much higher amount of alcohol or drugs in order to achieve intoxication or a desired effect, or I have a markedly diminished effect with continued use of same amount, than I did when I was younger.*

You may immediately recognize some of the problems that you already have—and remember, no excuse is a good excuse. So accept that you have these problems and don't put yourself down.

You are never a louse for giving yourself problems, and you can fully acknowledge their harmful consequences without upsetting yourself.

Rational Self-Statements

The following are some Rational Self-Statements you can repeat to yourself to help acknowledge your drinking problems, as well as to help bring about solutions. They are designed to help you face your problems without putting yourself down:

I have ignored my problems for a long time, but I can begin to face them now.

I do hurt myself with drinking, but I am not a louse for doing it.

I do make mistakes—all people make mistakes—I can face mine and I can manage them.

I am a fallible human being, but I can change myself.

Even though I hurt myself, I can fully accept myself.

My drinking sometimes creates problems for others, and that creates problems for me.

Any time my drinking gives me hassles, it's a problem.

Conclusion

In this chapter, we've been trying to show you that you have problems created by drinking or drug use, which is sort of like telling you that your car isn't running right when you don t see anything wrong with it. Without recognizing a problem, you will not do anything about it.

What can you do when you recognize that you have problems with drinking? Admit that you do not like having them and that you'll do better without them. Forgive yourself and accept yourself as a fallible human being who is capable of making mistakes.

Once you do this, you can feel appropriately regretful or sorrowful for your mistakes. If you want to change what you did to bring on these problems, you can look at the thoughts, emotions, and behaviors that have kept you drinking.

Next, you can quit drinking and begin to plan how you will enjoy yourself without depending on alcohol. Then, get started—do it! If you fail to follow through, you can still continue to accept yourself and continue to try. In REBT, we believe that if you face your drinking problems squarely and get rid of them, you will have less misery, much more happiness, and a healthy, rational outlook for living!

3

How To Gain a Realistic View of Your Drinking and Abstinence

Why would you ever think about quitting alcohol or drugs? Simply because you do not like some of the results of using them.

Once you see the bad results, why isn't it easy to quit? There can be many reasons: You like some of the results, especially those that occur quickly and easily such as the high, the good times, and the escapes from hassles. You may believe that you cannot stand doing without these effects (or the hope of them, because you may not be getting them now). And you may believe that because you have tried and failed to quit, you cannot quit and you're a failure who deserves nothing better than to be a drunk or druggie. Sometimes you may simply forget about the bad results. To cover up all these problems, you may create excuses: "I'm going to die from something, so it may as well be this," for example.

You can change these thinking problems. This book presents these problems, one at a time, and provides techniques designed to help you eliminate them. When you read and practice the techniques, you may find yourself doing better in your resolve to quit, or to stay quit, and in overcoming many emotional upsets as well.

This chapter, like the one before, is designed to help you increase your awareness of the problems caused by your drinking or drugging. It adds techniques to help you see some of the consequences of your behavior. You will see worksheets in this chapter that can help you identify both the advantages and disadvantages of drinking and sobriety. By using the worksheets and by concentrating on the problems and benefits of drinking (drugging) and quitting, you can think more realistically. And if your behavior has created serious problems and has significantly interfered with your long-term happiness, you may achieve greater motivation to quit.

Indeed, people who are successful at quitting think of the good and the bad of drinking (using): about what they get from drinking (using) and what may happen if they continue. In doing this, people often realize that they have not taken seriously the problems of drinking, and that they have exaggerated the benefits. When you think carefully about the items in the worksheet, and when you fill them out, you may begin to see that you also have not allowed yourself enough awareness of your drinking to allow you to make a sensible decision.

Our approach in REBT is very different from that of Alcoholics Anonymous. AA teaches that you must hit bottom and accept a Higher Power before you can quit. We believe people quit by changing their motivation, by making a commitment, and by following through.

People who decide to quit have one thing in common: they stop by wanting to and by developing an ability to do so if they do not already have it. Indeed, many people stop drinking (using) when they first discover problems. Others vacillate for months or even years. Still others want to quit, but continue drinking or using until their health and social well-being seriously deteriorate, and they reach a state of severe mental and physical impairment. But, nearly all quit only after developing a continuing awareness of good reasons to quit.

Here is the first worksheet in this chapter. Use it to develop awareness of the consequences of your behavior. Then respond to the items by writing in the space provided. Study them every day for at least three weeks and add to your answers as you study. If this book belongs to someone else, i.e., if you borrowed it from a library or friend, please do not write in it. Instead, copy these worksheets for yourself on a separate sheet of paper.

Worksheet I

Advantages/Disadvantages of Drinking and Sobriety

To use this worksheet, carefully read its items and consider your answers. Then, write your answers, think about them, and set them aside for awhile while you continue reading this book. You may find it helpful to read through the preceding chapter again. It might remind you of some problems. Frequently return to the worksheet to study it. This builds motivation. Now, let's begin:

Problems and Hassles With Drinking (Drugging)

Bad things (pains, problems, and hassles) that have happened to me as a result of my drinking (drugging) are:

Examples: Hangovers, problems with my family, late to work, being arrested for driving while intoxicated, getting upset at myself for drinking (using).

_____

_____

_____

_____

_____

The worst problem I ever had as a result of my drinking (drugging) was:

_____

_____

_____

If I continue to drink (take drugs), some bad things that can happen to me are:

_____

_____

_____

_____

_____

Good things that happen to me as a result of my drinking (drugging) are:

_____

_____

_____

_____

_____

The best thing drinking (drugging) ever did for me was:

_____

_____

_____

_____

I have given up on the following pleasures, goals, or dreams because my drinking (drugging) interfered:

_____

_____

_____

_____

What immediate pleasant activities can I enjoy that do not involve drinking (drugging)?

_____

_____

_____

_____

_____

What long-term goals can I accomplish if I quit drinking (drugging)?

_____

_____

_____

_____

_____

Worksheet II

Using the Referenting Technique

This worksheet uses a technique called referenting. When you think of an act, your thoughts about it may be both good and bad. For instance, when you think of drinking, you may think of relaxation, friends, and good times. And when you think of quitting, you may think of boredom and loss of enjoyment. When this occurs, it's easy to see why you don't quit. If you change these thoughts, you can have a different view of drinking (drugging) and quitting. To help you have a more complete view of drinking, drugging and quitting, read the following questions and think carefully about your answers. Then, follow the directions for Worksheet I.

When I think of quitting, what am I thinking that makes quitting seem bad?

Examples: I think of boredom, pain, and misery. I think of sleeplessness, anxiety, and doing worse in many ways.

When I think of drinking (drugging), what do I think of that makes drinking (drugging) seem good?

Examples: I think of regaining the best high, and I think of relaxing, feeling good, and having a good time.

When I want to quit drinking (drugging), what can I think that makes quitting seem good?

Examples: I can think of feeling better after a short while. And I can think of managing my problems, having less trouble, feeling happier, making fewer excuses, and living longer.

_____

_____

_____

_____

_____

When I seriously think about quitting, what can I think of drinking (drugging) that makes it seem bad?

Examples: Feeling fatigued, losing my job and/or my marriage, and dying sooner.

_____

_____

_____

_____

_____

Now, you can have more realistic beliefs about drinking (drugging) and quitting. By looking at the consequences, you can see your behavior for what it is, including both the good and the bad. However, you can easily forget this new knowledge. It can be compared to the gains attained through physical exercise—use it or lose it! To strengthen and maintain your realistic beliefs and feelings, think about the good and bad of drinking (drugging) again and again. The following are some suggestions to assist you:

Work Deliberately and Repetitively: Review your worksheets regularly. Establish a regular time to study them—say first thing in the morning, every day for three weeks—and think of your answers several times throughout the day. When you do, see if you notice a difference in how you think about drinking (drugging).

Make a Commitment to Yourself: If you have decided to quit, make a commitment. Vow to yourself that you will never drink (use) again. By making a commitment, you set a clear goal for yourself and you will have fewer problems with quitting. Here are several commitments that can help:

- To refrain from drinking (using).
- To accept that you will have urges to drink (use) that you will face, and that you will not give in to them.
- To work daily on reading self-help books such as this one and to do exercises that will help you mentally and emotionally.
- To work on immediate problems that drinking (drugging) has created and to pay attention to the responsibilities that you have neglected.
- To handle your stress appropriately.
- To enjoy what you can without drinking.
- To participate in more long-term, pleasant activities.
- To continue trying if you drink or use again.

Persist: Frequently remind yourself of the good and bad of drinking (drugging) and quitting. Then you can know more clearly what you want to do. If you are like many others, you will work at quitting for a long time after you first think about it seriously. You don't have to; you can quit right now. But, you may go back and forth about it. Rereading both this chapter and the one before, and using the techniques in them, can help you firmly establish your reasons to quit.

Keep Trying: You may think of a commitment as all-or-nothing: either you follow through or you do not, and if you do not, you have failed completely. This is not the case! If you fail, you may still succeed if you keep trying. That's the way others do it. Your commitment is merely a way to firmly establish your goals by making a vow to keep them. It is important to make such a commitment. If you fail to keep it, make another and work to keep it. Like others, you may then succeed.

Change Your Behavior

In REBT, we advise not only changing your thinking, but also changing your behavior. If you have decided to quit, follow through with your commitment by acting as if you have quit. Here are suggestions that may help:

Avoid People and Places Where You Drink: Give yourself a break from temptation. Avoid activities and places where you engage in drinking (using). To help yourself with this, spend time and effort on new activities. (Chapter 17, on happiness, can help with this.)

Work on Immediate Problems: Work on any immediate problems that you have neglected. You may have problems with your mate, children, employer, or the courts. Analyze your problems, concentrate on them, and work hard at solving them.

Find Something Better To Do: Think of an activity that does not involve drinking. Imagine yourself doing it—think of its benefits and pleasures. Then do it! Get involved! Absorb yourself in the activity for a while—even for a long time. (Chapter 17 can help you with this.)

Rational Self-Statements

The following are Rational Self-Statements that can help to motivate you. After reading the list, you can choose those that help, and you can develop others on your own. Then repeat them and use them to remind yourself of the many good reasons for quitting.

It is good for me to think carefully about the consequences of my drinking.

Although it is hard, I can think about my drinking.

Quitting will give me better health and more happiness.

Trying to quit and failing is better than failing to try.

When I think of alcohol or drugs, I can remember that they do not give me much.

Working at motivating myself is hard, but it's not too hard.

I'll make a commitment to myself and I'll work to keep it.

If I relapse, I'll commit again and I'll try again.

Conclusion

Use the worksheets to develop your ability to go in the direction that is right for you. Continuing to use them will help you even more. They can help you to work at thinking realistically about your drinking (or using) and quitting, especially the pleasures and pains that motivate you.

You may have felt concerned about your problems for years and even tried to quit. However, you may have also given yourself reasons to continue by exaggerating the benefits and down playing the detriments of drinking or using. These worksheets allow you to approach the idea of quitting in a deliberate, reasonable manner, and you may quit with only the help they give you. If not, the rest of the book contains information to help you deal with some roadblocks you may encounter.

It is wise to remember that if you want to quit, quitting is a decision and takes commitment. As stated often and for good reason, quitting is a process that takes work and practice. With persistent effort you can succeed. So, keep working—you can do it!

In the next few chapters, we offer something quite different from what we've presented thus far. We present the theory of Rational Emotive Behavior Therapy, its ideas about thinking, emotions and behavior, and we will present its theory on addictions. The theory will help you understand much about "what makes you tick," especially what goes wrong when you are doing badly. That's one of the main benefits of REBT's theory: It shows you what's going wrong with your thinking when you are not reaching your goals. Later, we will show you how to diagnose your problems, and how to fix them.

4

How Thinking Affects Emotions and Behavior

When you are struggling to quit drinking, how can Rational Emotive Behavior Therapy (REBT) help you? It can help you gain more control over your behavior by teaching you to think better, to feel better, and to act accordingly.

Albert Ellis founded REBT in 1955, when no widely accepted theory of psychotherapy stressed the importance of thinking in human emotions and behavior. He began REBT after he became discontented with the predominant psychoanalytic theory, and he based it on several sources: his studies in philosophy (that he began as a teenager); relatively new findings in behavioral research; and his experience helping people through straightforward, common-sense counseling.

In the early 1960s, other professionals began teaching principles similar to REBT, and today, cognitive (thinking) behavior therapy is one of the major approaches to psychotherapy and behavior change.

What role does thinking play in your behavior? In REBT, thoughts, emotions, and behavior are believed to be closely related most of the time. When you act, you have a goal—usually either happiness or less pain. You think of what you want, you feel an emotion, and you act. For instance, let's say that you are sitting in your easy chair reading, and you decide to do something different, such as watching television. First, you think, "I'm tired of reading —I prefer to watch television." Then, you put down your book and you turn on the TV. You go from the first activity to the second because you think of the second, you feel a desire, and you follow through by doing it.

When you drink or use, you also think before you act. You may think something like, "I want a drink," or "I need a drink." You may have little awareness of this thinking. You focus more on the effect of the booze or drugs than on the thoughts that lead you to drink or use, and the effect is what you know and remember. Because you are now trying to change your behavior and because you now know it is difficult, REBT teaches that you will do well to develop a greater appreciation of the thinking that leads you to drink or use and how you can change it.

When you try to change your behavior, as when you try to quit, your thinking affects how well you do. When you decide not to drink or use, you have rational thinking, beliefs that help you. You may think, "I want one, but, if I quit, I'll do better: I'll keep my job, my good health, and my marriage." With such beliefs you will feel good about quitting, and you will quit. You won't feel completely good, however, because you will be giving up drinking or drugging, which you do like. All things considered, though, you will feel mostly good.

That's simple, right? Then why don't you just quit for good? Because, you are not simple, and you waiver in your thinking and your commitment. After making your commitment, you easily think irrational beliefs, thoughts that can sabotage your decision to quit. You may think: "I need a drink (or a hit); it's too hard to quit; and I can't stand life without it." This irrational thinking can give you a strong urge which makes abstaining difficult, and you may strongly embrace those beliefs, thinking they are accurate and reflect exactly the way things are, so it's foolish to quit.

Al provides a good example. He tried to quit, and he did well throughout most of the day. But he had difficulties just before five o'clock, when he usually began to drink. His thinking went from commitment to ambivalence. His ambivalence began when he thought, "I always start drinking at five o'clock. It's too hard to give it up. Now's the time!" Then he thought, "But drinking gives me problems." Next, he thought, "I have worked so hard, I deserve a drink." Then, "But, I want to quit; I've had enough."

He argued with himself, going back and forth, back and forth, until he took a drink. What swayed him? He upset himself at the hassles he was giving himself by thinking, "This is too much of a hassle; I need a drink." He gave in and he drank.

If Al had eliminated his irrational thinking, most likely he would have remained abstinent. REBT tries to help you do just that. In later chapters, we explain how REBT can help you to get rid of your irrational beliefs. First, let's look at some of the differences between rational and irrational thinking as REBT defines it.

Differences Between Rational and Irrational Thinking

Rational thinking is defined in REBT as thinking that helps you achieve your goals, and irrational thinking is thinking that easily defeats you. Because you are human, you can easily go from rational thinking to irrational, for instance, from "I want what I want" to "I must have what I want."

Gaining awareness of your irrational thinking is an important step in helping yourself. Let's look now at the main irrational beliefs that people hold.

The main irrational belief is *should, ought*, or *must*. Wanting is good, but when you think you must have what you want, you create misery and you easily sabotage your ability to achieve your goals. The tendency of humans to think disturbing musts is so prevalent and so self-defeating that Albert Ellis coined the word *musturbation* (a combination of the words "must" and "disturb") to emphasize its importance.

One of the main characteristics of disturbing musts is that they are absolutistic and unconditional. Rational beliefs, by comparison, are non-absolutistic and conditional. When you rationally think, "I want a drink," you focus on a positive consequence such as relaxation, feeling comfortable, or feeling high. But if you've had problems with drinking, you will also think of the problems, such as losing your marriage, your job, and your good health. In contrast, when you add the irrational belief, "I need a drink," you mean "no ifs, ands, or buts," and you give less thought to the effects of drinking. You do not think of the consequences of drinking. So, rational thinking has distinct advantages over irrational thinking by allowing you a more realistic view of your decision-making processes and behavior.

Often, irrational thinking is not only absolutistic but illogical. You may think, for instance, "Because I had one drink, I'm doomed to be a drunk." It is true that you had a drink, but it does not follow that you are doomed to keep drinking. Many people slip up and have a drink without resuming drunkenness. Thus, your statement may seem logical, but when you look at it closely, you can see that it isn't.

Other Common Irrational Beliefs

There are many forms of irrational thinking, and the main characteristic, again, is that they contain an absolutistic and unconditional *must*. Let's look now at other common irrational beliefs that contain hidden musts with some examples both related to drinking and using and to your other behaviors.

Awful, Horrible, and Terrible: These beliefs usually mean worse than bad or more than 100% bad. Bad means having what you do not want, and things can get very bad. *Awful,* however, means worse than what you do not want, which does not exist as far as we mortal humans can prove.

Nothing in reality, we believe, can be worse than your dislike of it. You dislike some things more than others, but disliking something still means, simply, that you do not like it.

Because there are only varying degrees of badness and dislikes, and because there is nothing worse than (very) bad, then awful, horrible, or terrible do not exist.

Can't Stand: Can't stand is a primary irrational belief in creating low frustration tolerance, your tendency to give up when life gets tough. You may believe, for example, that you can't stand life without booze or drugs, when, in actuality, you only dislike it, and that may be only for awhile. Yes, life is tough and you do dislike some aspects of it, but it's possible to strongly dislike it when it's very bad without believing you can't stand it. According to REBT, you will do better, much better, when you only dislike difficulty and do not believe you cannot stand it.

All-or-Nothing/Always-or-Never: All-or-nothing thinking is also irrational. Examples are: "I'll always fail," and "If I have one drink, I have to go all the way because there is no in between for people like me." Examples not related to booze or drugs are, "You always criticize me," "You never treat me with respect," and "I'm never right."

When you think *all or nothing/always or never*, you narrowly focus on one aspect of behavior and take it too seriously; and you easily neglect all of the others. You leave out the middle where most of life occurs. For example, you may believe that you either completely succeed or you totally fail, when neither is the case. Usually, instead, you get some things right and some things wrong. You may believe that people can never be trusted when, much of the time, if you are truthful with yourself, you'll see that they treat you honestly most of the time.

I'm No Good/You're No Good: Putting yourself down and putting others down is also self-defeating. You and others may act badly, but these actions do not make you bad. For example, you may believe that if you failed to quit you're no good.

Rating people, including yourself, easily contributes to having problems both in your relationships and in achieving your individual goals. When you put yourself down, you easily feel anxious and shameful and you do poorly at learning from mistakes; when you put others down, you easily focus on their bad behavior and ignore the good, you often fail to learn from their mistakes, and you may break off relationships unnecessarily.

Rating *behavior* as either good or bad, without rating the *person*, allows you to do better. Then you can see both the good and the bad in both you and others without becoming upset at the total person.

I Can't: You may think, "Because I must do well, and I have failed many times, I absolutely *can't* do it." Does failure prove you absolutely can't succeed? No it doesn't. Usually it only proves that your method did not work and that you will do better to try another approach.

Need: Need means, "I must have what I want." For instance, many people believe they need a drink, when they only want one. In REBT, we believe that we cannot prove that needs exist, and that we have only wants and desires.

Deserve: When people think that they unconditionally deserve what they want, they often believe that events should be arranged for their benefit. You may think, "Because I've done the right thing, I absolutely should have special privileges; the world owes it to me, and it's a lousy rotten world if it doesn't give me what I want." This kind of thinking is not only absolutistic, illogical, and impractical, but it just doesn't fit with the way the world works. Do you ever absolutely deserve anything? No! Think about it. You like to get what you want, but nothing in the universe says that you *must* get you want.

As previously mentioned, these irrational beliefs usually contain absolutistic musts. For example, if you only believe you don't *want* to be deprived of alcohol, would you then believe that life without it is *awful?* Usually not. If you believe, however, that you *must* not be deprived, you can easily think that abstinence is *awful*.

If you only don't want discomfort, would you then believe that you "can't stand it?" Probably not. You may, however, think that you "can't stand it" when you believe that you *must* not have discomfort.

The above examples of irrational thinking are among the most common, and they can easily hinder you in achieving your goals. How do they defeat you? They easily lead you to exaggerate, to feel miserable and compelled, and to overly focus on difficulty and hardship and away from your own happiness and survival.

When you tell yourself you *need* a drink (a hit), you exaggerate its benefits and you feel compelled to have one, making it exceptionally hard not to take a drink (or to use), and you easily neglect the long term harm it does to you. However, when you rationally tell yourself that you *want* a drink, you may feel a desire for a drink, but you have more of a choice in refusing to have one because you can see the big picture, including the harmful results of drinking.

Conclusion

Thinking, whether irrational or rational, leads you to act. Identifying your irrational thinking and developing a greater awareness is important in your decision to stop drinking or using, as well as in your ability to follow through with that decision. When you learn to recognize your irrational thinking, you will find some of these common irrational beliefs again and again. Acknowledging them can help you understand both your problem behavior and emotions and how they defeat you.

Since the primary irrational belief is *must*, when you have beliefs that include absolutistic and unconditional musts, such as, "I need a drink," or "I can't stand living without booze," you easily defeat yourself by feeling miserable and by acting irrationally. REBT teaches you how to eliminate the irrational beliefs that contribute to your drinking and drugging, leaving you with rational thinking that can help you quit; and it teaches you how to manage the problems that you face in remaining sober.

5

How to Understand Your Emotions

Most likely, you know that you sometimes drink to deal with your emotions. For instance, you may feel depressed, so you drink. And after quitting you may relapse by drinking to cope with an upset such as depression, anxiety, anger, or embarrassment. A key point in quitting is that you can learn to eliminate your emotional upsets without drinking. Rational Emotive Behavior Therapy (REBT) offers a precisely focused theory on emotions that can help you understand and change them.

We believe that you can have appropriate (helpful) or inappropriate (hindering) emotions. Appropriate emotions help you in attaining your goals, whereas inappropriate emotions (emotional upsets) easily defeat you. Inappropriate emotions are the ones that feel miserable when you want a drink and don't have it. Sometimes, people trying to quit will relapse when struggling with these emotions. Fortunately, you can nearly eliminate them. You probably won't completely eliminate them, but when you use our approach, you may diminish them so greatly that you only rarely give a thought to drinking.

In this chapter, we discuss the differences between helpful emotions and emotional upsets. In later chapters, we will show you how to eliminate them.

Appropriate and Inappropriate Emotions

Our view differs from the commonly held belief that emotions simply feel either good and bad. We believe you can feel bad without feeling upset, and your bad feelings can help you. You can feel frustrated, for instance, when you make a mistake, and that can help you to adjust and do better. Likewise, feeling good is not always helpful. You can feel prideful and grandiose, for instance, which feels good, but which can easily lead you to do less that makes you happy. So, instead of thinking of emotions as either good or bad, consider thinking of how they help you and how they hinder you.

Are emotions a sign of weakness, as many people think? Hardly. As you will see in further discussions, you do better with feelings than without them, and we advise you to appreciate all your emotions and to fully accept yourself along with them.

Consider the following illustration. Do you remember Michael Spinks, the boxer who won an Olympic gold medal in the 1970s and later the heavyweight title? During the Olympics, he won a bout against an opponent who had beaten him a year before. When asked why he lost before, he stated, "Because I wasn't afraid. Now, when I discover I don't fear someone [before a fight], I conjure up some [fear] because I'd rather be safe than sorry." Would you conclude from this that fear is an emotion to be avoided? No, of course not. Fear helped Michael Spinks and it can help you.

"I don't want to feel bad; I want to feel good. Why don't you teach me how to feel good?" We do, in Chapter 16 on frustration and Chapter 17 on happiness. But we know of no good way to quickly and easily feel good for the long run. With drinking and using, you have an easy escape from your misery, and you can attain an easy though short-term happiness. However, to gain long-term happiness with fewer problems and hassles, you do better to eliminate quick and easy emotional fixes. So quit copping out by drinking or using and work to face your problems and to acknowledge your upsets without panicking. By eliminating your upsets you will feel better. See for yourself just how differently these emotions can feel. Read the following two sets of beliefs and notice how you feel after reading each set:

Rational Beliefs

I failed; that's bad; it means I am fallible and I didn't get what I want.

I want what I want, and I don't like not getting it.

I want you to treat me better; if you don't, you have blundered.

I don't like so much work; it's a lot to do.

Irrational Beliefs

I failed; I didn't get what I want; that's awful; it means I am no good.

I need what I want, and I can't stand not getting it.

You must treat me better; if you don't, you're no good.

I can't stand so much work; it's too much.

The emotions aroused by these beliefs feel different, don't they? People holding the first set of beliefs usually feel helpfully bad while people holding the second set usually feel miserable or disturbed. We try to help you feel emotions aroused by the first set of beliefs, whereas, your disturbances are aroused by the second set of beliefs. By changing your emotions from disturbed to negative-but-helpful, we believe you can do better in life and, ultimately, feel happier.

How do emotions influence your actions? Consider sadness and depression. They affect your ability to follow through with a commitment to quit drinking (using).

First, let's look at depression. You may realize that you have some good reasons to quit, but you tell yourself, "I shouldn't have to stop drinking; I should be able to get away with it," and you become angry and depressed. How will you behave? You probably will not quit and you may drink even more.

On the other hand, you may feel sad; and if you hold a rational belief, such as, "I don't like giving up alcohol; but I can stand it," how will you behave? You may find it easier to stay straight because you are thinking sensibly about it, even though you do not feel entirely good about it, and you can bear the difficulties more easily because you will not overly focus on feeling deprived. Then, you can rationally consider the benefits you can attain without drinking.

To gain a better understanding of differences between helpful and hindering emotions, let's use a hypothetical situation and focus on the effects of emotions. In particular, we will look at some differences between annoyance, which can be helpful, and anger, which is usually hindering. Let's say that you want to see a movie this weekend and are reading the movie reviews. As you read, you feel good about some and not so good about others. Your emotions help you decide which of the movies you want to see. Your bad feelings help as well as your good feelings. If you had no emotions, you could not decide as well. Can you imagine feeling only good about the movies you like and not feeling bad about the movies you dislike? That would not be realistic.

Let's say it's now Friday night and that you go to the movie with some friends. When you arrive, you look at the marquis and see the title of another movie and not the one you want to see. You feel bad, disappointed. As before, can you imagine having no emotions? Don't you want to feel bad if they are showing a movie that you do not want to see?

Then, you feel helpfully annoyed by thinking, "They made a stupid mistake; that's lousy." How will this emotion help you? It can help you take useful action. You can talk to the manager and inform him of the error. This can help prevent it from happening again, which is good. You can think more flexibly about what to do next by thinking the rational belief, "I wanted to enjoy myself, and I still do. Since they are not showing the movie I want to see, I wonder what else I can do for fun?"

On the other hand, let's say you add anger to your annoyance. You think, "They shouldn't have made such a stupid mistake; they're no damn good for causing me such a hassle; they shouldn't be allowed to get away with this." Will your anger help you to take beneficial actions? Very probably not, especially when compared with annoyance. With anger, you could argue with the manager which could turn out badly, and you could do worse—

you could provoke a fight. Then you might feel guilty about fighting. Finally, your behavior might affect the happiness of both you and the people around you. All of this is bad. You started out enjoying yourself, but you ruined the evening by becoming angry.

The situation is bad enough, right? However, you could do worse still. You could tell yourself, "I can't take this; I need a drink." Here you upset yourself about your anger, feel miserable, believe you must relieve your stress, and turn all of this into an excuse to drink—a real cop-out. With that, not only do you sabotage the happiness you planned for the evening, but you think of getting drunk, a lousy way of handling your problems.

Why not just work at eliminating your anger so you only feel annoyed? It's a lot easier and healthier in the long run. With annoyance you can either correct the bad situation or accept it (if you can't change it), and then move on. That's much better!

In the above example, many people would say that the situation created the anger. However, in REBT, we believe people create their own anger. How? With their thinking about the situation. If, while you drive down the highway, you feel rage at a careless driver, you may believe the other driver causes your rage. If your mate acts badly and you get angry, you may believe he or she causes your anger. According to REBT, however, the event is not the cause of your disturbance. Why?

Think about it. If events cause emotional disturbances, then all people would get similarly disturbed by similar particular events, but this is not the case. All people do not get upset. Different people have different responses. If events cause upsets, when the events stop, the upsets will stop. Again, this is not the case. Many people remain upset long after events have passed. If events cause emotional disturbances, then you will never become upset until an event occurs. But, again, this is not the case. Many people become upset before an event occurs, by thinking about it. Most importantly, if events cause your emotional upsets, you will not be able to change your emotions and adjust. But many people do. Indeed, as the ancient philosopher Epictetus taught, people are not disturbed by events but by the beliefs they have about them.

There are distinct advantages to this approach. If you try to change both the problems in the world and the problems in your thinking, you will find it's easier to change your thinking. So, if you'd spend a year working on your thinking instead of changing the world, you would accomplish much more for yourself. The world and its events can, at the worst, give you only extreme unhappiness, whereas your thinking can give you misery. If given the choice of either unhappiness or misery, most people would take unhappiness.

Another common question is, "If you learn to think more rationally, will you become an emotionless robot?" No. The results of good REBT allow you more helpful emotions that are free of disturbances. You can feel more, not less. When you feel strongly without feeling upset, you can work better at eliminating problems and gaining enjoyment. So, you will not only feel better without your upsets, you can do better. For example, Craig Larsen, whose story is presented in Chapter 1, said that after overcoming his anxiety and depression, he had many other feelings, including sadness, regret, and concern, as well as happiness.

The Primary Emotions

You can help yourself greatly by identifying your emotions, especially when you upset yourself. The following are the primary appropriate (helpful) and inappropriate (hindering) emotions:

Emotions About You

Appropriate (helpful)—Concern and Regret: Concern is helpful. You may feel concerned when you think that you may fail or be rejected, or when you want to prevent problems or mistakes. You may think, "I want to do well and gain the approval of others, but it's possible that I won't." This will create the emotion of concern. Similarly, regret is an appropriate emotion you may have when you consider your past mistakes and think, "I wish I had acted differently—if I had, things would have turned out better."

Inappropriate (hindering)—Anxiety, Guilt, and Shame: With anxiety, you may excessively concern yourself about doing well or gaining approval. Examples: "I must do well and get the approval of people who are important to me; something unfortunate can occur, and I must be able to handle it well; if I don't I'll be worthless," and, "I must be in control; it would be awful if things go wrong; I can't stand it when bad things happen."

With guilt, you may put yourself down for doing something badly, such as harming someone or not fitting into society's norms. Examples: "I should not have acted wrongly; I do not have the good characteristics that others value, and I should," and, "I should have done better; I'm worthless for the mistakes I've made and I should be condemned and punished."

A common question that people ask is, "If I hurt someone, shouldn't I feel guilty?" No. In REBT, we believe guilt hinders you from learning from your mistakes and from correcting them. With guilt, you feel miserable and you can spend enormous amounts of time and energy condemning yourself, which will not help you change. You not only feel worse, you easily do worse. Feeling regret for your mistakes is better. With regret, you feel helpfully sorry; you can apologize to the wronged person, and you may succeed when you try to rectify your mistake. You can learn from your mistake, put it behind you, and move on. On the other hand, with guilt, you will usually continue to feel miserable, and you may never change the behavior that led you to do badly.

Shame is similar to guilt, although it involves your relations with others. With shame, you awfulize when others see your mistakes by thinking something like, "When others see that I have faults, which I *must not* have, it makes me a terrible person." With this emotion, you feel shy and you are overly afraid of others seeing your shortcomings. This often contributes to lack of intimacy with close friends, lack of assertiveness, and hesitancy to take risks in your work.

Emotions About Others

Appropriate (helpful)—Annoyance: This is an appropriate emotion you may feel when you dislike someone's behavior. You may think, "I don't like what you did, and you are definitely wrong to have done it."

With this emotion (annoyance) you can see that it was the person's act that was bad and not the total person; and you can still appreciate the good that they do. In many cases, you can tolerate the bad behavior of others and continue your relationship with them although you do not like all that they do.

Inappropriate (hindering)—Anger: Many people view anger as being "justified." In REBT, we believe anger easily sabotages your happiness and leads to many problems. Beliefs that can create anger are, "You should not treat me badly. You are damnable if you do; you should not frustrate me. Because I have done a lot for you, you should do as much for me." Feeling annoyed (see above) is usually better.

Emotions About Conditions of Daily Life

Appropriate (helpful)—Frustration and Sadness: Frustration is helpful. It helps you know when events are going wrong for you. When you feel frustrated you think of the things that get in your way, and you think, simply, something like, "I'm frustrated and I don't like it."

The events that frustrate you can be many and varied. Two examples are: 1) events that are external to you, such as rush hour traffic, long lines at the grocery store, and slow bureaucracies; and 2) your own human nature, such as your fallibility and the fact that changing yourself is difficult. Sadness is also helpful. You feel sad when you think, "It's unfortunate that I am not getting what I want."

With feelings of sadness and frustration, you can work constructively with life's difficulties. You can recognize when you do not have what you want. You can then work to change these events; and if you are not successful, you can then learn to tolerate it and work with it. For instance, you may want to change yourself quickly and easily, but you find that you cannot. At that point, you can decide to tolerate this frustration and work persistently at changing yourself over a period of time. You can then succeed, perhaps not as you wanted, but in the best way possible under the circumstances.

Inappropriate (hindering)—Depression (Low Frustration Tolerance): You make yourself depressed when you add absolutistic and unconditional demands to your frustrations. You can feel depressed when you think, "The world should give me what I want, quickly and easily; I can't stand it when things are hard; it's awful to have to put up with this difficult, rotten world." When you compare the kind of thinking that creates depression with the kind of thinking that creates feelings of sadness and frustration, you can see that depression adds misery to your frustrations. In addition, when you are depressed, you do not adjust well to ordinary hassles, which greatly handicaps you in doing anything worthwhile.

Conclusion

Sometimes you drink to cope with your emotions, and you may use your emotions as an excuse to drink. Nearly always, you will do better to quit drinking with the knowledge that your emotions are not a good excuse to drink, and then to work at better managing them. REBT offers you an efficient means of help that begins by recognizing important differences between your emotions: mainly that some are helpful and others are hindering.

You easily hinder yourself with anger, anxiety, and depression; and you help yourself with annoyance, concern, and frustration. After you quit drinking, you will be wise to work at eliminating your emotional upsets, which you can do with REBT's approach. Then, you will both feel better and, probably, gain more from living—much more than you did while drinking.

6

Rational Emotive Behavior Therapy's Theory on Addiction

So far we've presented Rational Emotive Behavior Therapy's (REBT) theory of irrational thinking and harmful emotions, and how they can defeat you. Does this theory provide insights into addiction? Yes it does. According to REBT, thinking and emotions have a great deal to do with how people addict themselves.

REBT's Theory on Addiction was developed by Albert Ellis, and it appears in the cassette tape Addictive Personalities, available through the Institute of Rational Emotive Therapy in New York City. This theory focuses mainly on the irrational beliefs and inappropriate emotions that play a role in the psychological aspects of addiction. It defines six levels of addiction and their varying aspects, allowing you to understand the processes of addiction. It also illustrates the progression of beliefs, emotions, and behaviors related to the severity of individuals' addictions.

Not all addicted people go through all of the levels, and some go through only a few. This theory can help you determine if you have addicted yourself and, if so, at which level.

Two Psychological Forms of Addiction

There are two forms of addiction, both involving irrational thinking and emotional disturbance. *Low Frustration Tolerance (LFT)* is the primary emotional disturbance in both forms. The first form, I refer to as *LFT-Related and Pleasure-Seeking Addiction*. It is a relatively simple form in which the primary emotional disturbance is Low Frustration Tolerance (LFT). The second I refer to as *Addiction Related to General Emotional Disturbance*. It's a more complicated form of addiction.

Low Frustration Tolerance and Pleasure-Seeking Addiction: People with the LFT-related type believe they must have the pleasurable substance or activity and they upset themselves at the thought of not having it. For instance, they may think that they have to continue drinking even though it's creating problems for them, because they believe they have to have the pleasure the substance gives them.

People with LFT-related addiction may also add secondary problems to their basic addiction. With these secondary problems, they upset themselves with their excessive drinking (using) by thinking something like, "I'm no good for drinking so much," thereby damning themselves. Or, they may think, "Drinking (using) should not create all these problems," and "It's awful that I'm so weak that I can't stop," thereby creating Low Frustration Tolerance about their addiction. Instead of dealing with these upsets directly, they cop out and drink or use, thereby doing little to help themselves while creating more problems with alcohol or drugs.

People with the Pleasure-Seeking type believe that they must have excitement and adventure in their lives and that they can't stand living an ordinary life. They may believe that they must have fun and excitement in their lives, that alcohol or drugs gives it to them, and so they must drink or use. They can also develop urges to continue when they think of giving up their substance.

Addiction Related to General Emotional Disturbance: As previously mentioned, this is the more complicated form of addiction involving six levels and Low Frustration Tolerance along with other emotional disturbances including guilt, anger, anxiety, and depression. Albert Ellis calls this *Disturbance-Related Addiction*. The different levels reflect a progression of addiction along with increasing complexity. Some people quit drinking or using in the early levels when they first recognize significant problems. Others continue to drink, advancing through the different levels— adding problem upon problem—and, eventually, develop severe social and health impairments. The degree of disturbance ranges from normal neurotic to severely disturbed. The amount of difficulty you may have in quitting, as well as in the recovery process, is influenced by the degree of the disturbance. Problems with emotional disturbance can precede drinking, and the reverse is also true: drinking can contribute to and precede emotional disturbance.

LEVEL ONE—*Emotional Disturbance:* At this level, you upset yourself like most other people. Emotional upsets that contribute to this form of addiction usually contain some form of the following three emotional disturbances that are common to nearly all people.

Upsets at Yourself: You upset yourself at yourself, thus creating the emotions of anxiety, guilt, and shame, as well as the behaviors of procrastination and shyness. The main irrational belief is:

I must do well and get the approval of others; it's awful to fail and to get rejected; I can't stand doing badly; I'm no good when I do poorly.

Upsets at the Actions of Others: When you make yourself upset at others, your main disturbance is anger. This upset can include vengeful or homicidal feelings sometimes leading to over-rebellion and violent acts. The main irrational beliefs are:

You (other people) must treat me nicely, kindly, and in just the way I want; I can't stand it when you act badly; it's awful to get treated badly by you; you're no good for treating me less kindly and considerately than I want.

Upsets at the Conditions of Daily Living: When you upset yourself at conditions in you daily life—usually discomfort and difficulty—your main disturbances include LFT, depression, and self-pity. These emotions easily contribute to the behavioral problems of procrastination, avoidance, and withdrawal. The main irrational belief is:

The world should arrange itself so I can get what I want quickly, easily, and with few hassles; I cannot tolerate it when I feel uncomfortable; it's awful to have difficulty; it is a rotten world that makes me work long and hard to get what I want.

LEVEL TWO—*Low Frustration Tolerance At Emotional Disturbance:* At this level of addiction, people upset themselves at their upsets, and use alcohol, drugs, or eating to cope with these upsets. The first disturbance we call the *Primary Upset* and it may include the three main emotional disturbances—anger, depression, and anxiety. We call the second disturbance, which is usually more disturbing than the first, the *Secondary Upset.* It usually includes LFT, created by an irrational belief such as, "I can't stand feeling depressed! " Then, to cope, a person who drinks would add one more irrational belief: "I need a drink!"

If you become confused by finding LFT in two forms of addiction, *LFT-Related* and *Addiction Related to General Emotional Disturbance,* it's important to know that LFT is a basic part of both types of addiction, but not the whole of them. LFT is a part of both, like water is a part of beer and iced tea, steel is a part of both a car's engine and hood, and flour a part of both bread and cake. In the first more simple form of addiction, it is a major part, but in the second, more complex, form of addiction, it is a smaller, but still important part.

Examples of Secondary Upsets (Upsets at Upsets) and Drinking (Using) to Cope: The following are three examples of Secondary Upsets (Upsets at Upsets). First is the Primary Upset, followed by the Secondary Upset.

Primary Upset—Anxiety, Shame: I must do well at giving this speech or else I'm a failure; if others see that I'm nervous, that would be awful; I can't take it when I make mistakes and look bad in front of others.

Secondary Upset—LFT: I can't take feeling so nervous; I need a drink in order to take the edge off.

Primary Upset—Anger: You are a lousy, no-good rotten person for treating me so badly; you must treat me better; your behavior is awful; I can't stand it!

Secondary Upset—LFT: I can't take this stress; I need a drink!

Primary Upset—LFT, Depression: It's too hard to manage so many problems; the world gives me too many hassles and that's awful; I can't stand it; the world's a lousy rotten place and not fit for people to live in.

Secondary Upset—LFT: I can't stand feeling depressed; I need a drink.

LEVEL THREE—*Rationalization and Denial:* True addiction begins here. People notice problems with their drinking and try to quit or to control their drinking, but they fail because of Low Frustration Tolerance. They may think, "It's too hard to quit; I must have the good feeling alcohol gives." At this point, they wisely acknowledge that they have a drinking (drug) problem and that they are responsible for it. Then they begin to think irrationally, creating inappropriate emotions of shame and self-hate. They may think, "I should be able to control my drinking; I'm no good because I can't drink like others; if others find out, that will be awful!" To manage the misery created by these irrational beliefs, they tend to make excuses for their behavior—they rationalize and/or deny their problems with beliefs such as, "I can quit any time I want to; everybody has a vice—this is mine." By trying and failing to manage their drinking (using), and then by thinking irrationally both about their failure and about themselves, they have addicted themselves.

LEVEL FOUR—*Acknowledgment of Your Addiction with Self-Damnation:* At this level, people rationally acknowledge their addiction, and then irrationally damn themselves for it. Here are examples of self-damning statements:

I'm a no-good failure for not controlling my drinking; I hate myself.

I'm a low-life for being a drunk.

Basically I'm no good anyway and my failure to control my drinking proves I'm no good.

A louse like me can't quit.

Holding these irrational beliefs easily results in your con-tinuing to drink, as well as damning yourself even more for drinking. This creates an even stronger addiction.

LEVEL FIVE—*The Vicious Circle and Hitting Bottom:* At this level, people go though a complex and continuing series of upsets, followed by drinking bouts, which produce a degenerative cycle along with an irrational state of thinking. They believe that it is impossible to control or quit drinking. During this cycle, a person eventually deteriorates to his most extreme state of psychological and physical impairment. How does it happen?

Time and again, they repeat this cycle. They make themselves upset and then become disturbed at their upset. They drink (use) to cope and they deny that they have a drinking (drug) problem. They acknowledge their addiction and damn themselves even more. This increases their level of disturbance and they drink (use) compulsively to deal with self-damnation. The alcohol may impair their brain functioning. They may lose their job, their mate and their friends; and their physician may tell them that they are killing themselves with alcohol. But, they still don't quit! Instead, they make excuses. They may tell themselves: "I didn't like my boss anyway, my spouse was just a big pain, and I'll meet new friends at the bar—so good riddance! Not only that, I'll beat the doctor by proving her wrong!" They have completed the vicious cycle and will now either repeat it, degenerating mentally and physically until the alcohol kills them, or they will hit bottom by quitting and beginning their recovery. This is the final stage in the deterioration process of addiction.

LEVEL SIX—*Temptation with Tendency to Relapse:* When people finally make the decision to quit drinking, they are faced with many temptations and obstacles. They can be confronted with thoughts, emotions, and circumstances associated with old patterns of drinking (using). These temptations make abstinence difficult, and continuing these old habits is much easier than developing new ones. So relapse is much easier than abstinence.

They may also have other problems that create temptations and tendencies to relapse—including strong irrational beliefs, upsets about upsets, and the irrational belief that they must feel better immediately. When they decide to quit, they may think about the pleasures of drinking (using) and not about the long-term consequences. They may find sobriety to be boring, they may tend to look for excitement, and they may think that they will have to work forever at being sober. Because of this, they set unrealistic demands for themselves, such as never drinking (using) again, thus failing to allow for their human fallibility. Finally, they may become preoccupied with immediate concerns and events while losing sight of the advantages of sobriety. These are just a few of the reason people are tempted to relapse into drinking again.

Summary

There are two main forms of addiction. The first mainly involves Low Frustration Tolerance (LFT), and the other is more complex and involves general emotional disturbance.

A. *Low Frustration Tolerance and Pleasure-Seeking Addiction:* This relatively simple form of addiction is usually related to LFT and pleasure seeking. You demand the benefits of alcohol or other substances and have poor tolerance for doing without.

B. *General Emotional Disturbance:* This form of addiction involves many levels and may include nearly all forms of emotional disturbance. The levels are as follows:

Level One—*General Emotional Disturbance:* This level includes emotional upsets at yourself, others, and conditions of daily living, i.e., anxiety, anger, and depression.

Level Two—*Low Frustration Tolerance at Neurotic Disturbance:* At this level, you upset yourself about your upsets and use a substance to cope.

Level Three—*Rationalization and Denial:* Here you admit you have a drinking problem, try to quit and fail, damn yourself for drinking, and make excuses for it.

Level Four—*Acknowledgment of Your Addiction with Self-Damnation:* You admit your addiction, and you strongly damn yourself.

Level Five—*The Vicious Circle and Hitting Bottom:* You make yourself upset at your drinking (using), and you drink (use) to cope with your upset. You do this repeatedly until you either die from alcohol-related illnesses or you quit drinking.

Level Six—*Temptation With Tendency to Relapse:* After you quit, you have many temptations and become upset with the temptations.

How To Begin

With the many problems you have with your drinking, you may ask, "How do I begin?" With the simpler forms of addiction, LFT-related and Pleasure Seeking, work at eliminating the use of alcohol (or drugs) to manage your Low Frustration Tolerance and as a form of seeking pleasure, and then work at eliminating any remaining problems you may have.

With the more complex form of addiction, Addiction Related to General Emotional Disturbance, we recommend that you first find the level of your addiction (Levels One–Six), and then work at managing and overcoming your problems at that level. Then, progress to the next lower level. For example, if you see yourself at Level Three, focus and work on those problems, and then go to Level Two.

Conclusion

REBT's theory on addiction can help you discover many of the problems involved with your drinking or using of substances, including whether or not you have addicted yourself and, if so, how. With this theory, you have a plan, a map, to guide you, so you will know where to begin to attain sobriety as well as the direction in which to go. You can see where you have been, where you are, and where you are going!

7

Discovering Your Irrational Beliefs and Changing Them

Change is hard, especially when you don't know how to go about it. Rational Emotive Behavior Therapy (REBT) uses sensible procedures designed to help you gain awareness of yourself along with an ability to alter your behavior. It focuses on irrational thinking as the main part of you that you can identify and change. REBT uses two primary techniques to help you identify and eliminate your irrational beliefs. They are the *ABCs* and *Disputing Irrational Beliefs (DIBs)*. The ABCs help you examine your emotional upsets by focusing on your thoughts, emotions, and behaviors, thereby helping you recognize your irrational thinking. After gaining awareness of your irrational Beliefs, you can begin eliminating them by disputing them. Practicing these techniques frees you to change how you act, allowing you to chip away at problem behaviors like addiction.

Discover Your Irrational Beliefs

The ABCs of REBT allow you to analyze almost any upset that you have. They help you to clearly focus on your thoughts, emotions, and behaviors that create an emotional upset, which is a self-created state in which you easily defeat yourself.

Just what is an A, a B, and a C in this technique? An A is an *Activating event*—an event that blocks you from attaining what you want. The B is your *Belief*—usually about the A, and the C is the

Consequence—the emotional and behavioral reaction.

Mike provides a good illustration of how to use the ABCs. He was an Orlando S.M.A.R.T. Recovery group member who tried and failed to quit drinking. He told us, "I don't think I can quit." We did the ABCs by first looking for the A (Activating event) by asking, "What is the event at which you became upset?" "I don't know," he said. Another member responded, "I know; you tried to quit and you failed. Is that right?" Mike agreed. His A was "I failed at quitting."

Next we asked for the C, his Consequent feelings and behavior: "How did you feel and how did you act when you failed?" Mike thought a few seconds and replied, "I became depressed and I kept failing." So failure and depression were his Cs.

To get to the B, his Belief about the A, we asked, "What are you telling yourself about failing that makes you feel depressed and to continue failing?" He answered, "Because I have tried to quit and I have failed, I can't quit."

By doing the ABCs with Mike, he was able to identify and to clearly focus on the main source of his upset—his irrational thinking. That is the beginning of changing yourself with REBT.

Here is another illustration of how to use the ABCs to identify an emotional upset. Say you have an argument with your spouse. You decide to use the ABCs to better understand your behavior. First, you think of the A—the Activating event—and you discover that your spouse started the argument when you came home late. Then you consider what your emotions were—what you felt—about the A. You realize your emotional Consequence (eC) was anger. Next, you focus on your self-defeating act—your behavioral Consequence (bC)—which was to argue with your spouse in return. Next you discover your Bs, your Beliefs, by asking yourself, "What did I tell myself about my spouse's behavior that made me feel intolerant, angry, and argumentative?" You discover, "My spouse shouldn't start an argument; I can't stand arguing; it's awful; I have to stop her." These are your irrational Beliefs.

We have completed two illustrations using the ABCs—one related to problems with giving up drinking, and the other regarding a marital problem. With the ABCs, we discovered some irrational beliefs. Let's go now to more specific information to help you use this technique.

What are As (Activating events)? They can be anything you dislike. They can be your thoughts, emotions and actions or the actions of other people, (usually how they treat you). You may also upset yourself at the problems and hassles of daily living, usually the difficulties you have. To discover your A, ask yourself, "What is the event that I am I upsetting myself about?"

What are Cs, Consequent emotions or behaviors?

Emotional Cs (eCs) can be anxiety, guilt, shame, depression, and anger. Behavioral Cs (bCs) can be drinking (using), avoiding responsibilities, procrastination, and arguing. To discover your C, ask yourself, "How am I feeling about the A?" or "What action did I take in response to the A that turned out badly?"

What are irrational Beliefs? Usually they are statements of wants or preferences containing absolutistic thinking such as the following: should, ought, must, have to, can't stand, awful, horrible, terrible, always or never, I absolutely can't, I'm no good and you're no good. Examples are: "I *must* do well," and "Getting what I want *should* be easy." To discover your Bs, try asking yourself, "What am I telling myself about the A (event) that creates my C (emotion)?" Specifically, you can ask questions such as the following:

What am I telling myself about my urge that creates a desperate feeling?

What am I telling myself about quitting that creates my helpless feeling?

What am I telling myself about my drinking that creates my feelings of guilt and shame?

What am I telling myself about my failure that leads me to quit trying?

By doing the ABCs you can quickly determine why you feel and act as you do when you defeat yourself. We are ready now for Disputing Irrational Beliefs or DIBs, the primary technique that helps you change.

Using DIBs to Eliminate Irrational Beliefs

When you've repeatedly tried and failed to quit drinking, the theory of REBT states that an irrational Belief contributed to your failure. It may not be all that led to failure, but we believe it's a significant part. After you discover the irrational Belief, you can work to change it and your self-defeating behavior.

Disputing Irrational Beliefs or DIBs is the most common way of eliminating irrational Beliefs used in REBT. With DIBs, you challenge your Beliefs by looking for evidence that they are true. Your Belief may be, "I must do well at quitting." You may challenge this Belief with, "Prove it. Where's the evidence?" Challenging irrational Beliefs shows you that they cannot be proven; thus Disputing helps you change. If your Beliefs make sense, keep them. If they do not, you can begin to give them up.

When you continue to Dispute your irrational Beliefs, you can make yourself less prone to disturbance, so that you may never become extremely upset (self-defeating) again. You can make profound and lasting changes with Disputing coupled with working to change your behaviors.

This approach is authoritative, not authoritarian. With these techniques you can discover for yourself if your Beliefs are true, and you can change your Beliefs only when you see that they do not make sense. In this way, you can help yourself independently of experts.

Here is an example of Disputing that entails the use of four disputing questions.

iB (irrational Belief): I need a drink; it's *awful* to deprive myself; I *can't stand it.*

Disputing Question # 1: Is there any evidence my Belief is true?

E (Effective New Belief): No! I can prove that I *want* a drink, but not that I absolutely *need* a drink. I can prove that it will feel bad to deprive myself, but I can't prove that it's *awful.* I can prove that I don't *like* depriving myself, but I can't prove that I *can't stand it.*

Disputing Question # 2: Is there any evidence my Belief is false?

E (Effective New Belief): Yes! I have deprived myself of a drink in the past and I was able to stand it, because I survived. It was bad, but only bad. Other people live without alcohol, and they do okay. Therefore, I can too. Finally, there was a time when I didn't drink at all, and I did fine.

Disputing Question # 3: What good can happen, or what good can I make happen, if I give up my Belief?

E (Effective New Belief): If I give up my irrational Belief, I can find it easier to quit drinking. I won't think of alcohol as much, and I won't feel as compelled and desperate.

Disputing Question # 4: What bad can happen, or what bad can I easily make happen, if I keep my Belief?

E (Effective New Belief): It will be hard to quit because I will feel desperate at feeling deprived, and I may continue to drink, giving me even more problems.

Remember the hypothetical argument with your spouse earlier in this chapter? The following is a Dispute of an irrational Belief we found in that illustration. It shows how you can use DIBs with problems not related to drinking:

iB: My spouse shouldn't start an argument; I can't stand arguing; it's awful, so I have to stop her.

Disputing Question # 1: Is there any evidence my Belief is true?

E (Effective New Belief): No! I can prove I don't like her behavior. I can prove that it is bad and that I want her to quit, but I can't prove any shoulds, can't stands, awfuls, or have tos.

Disputing Question # 2: Is there any evidence my Belief is false?

E (Effective New Belief): Yes! My spouse did start an argument, and it is bad that she did. Even though I do not like it, I will survive her behavior, and I will probably survive similar behavior in the future. Even though I would like to have more influence, I can tolerate my spouse's behavior without any bad consequences.

Disputing Question # 3: What good can happen, or what good can I make happen, if I give up my Belief?

E (Effective New Belief): If I give up my Belief, I can tolerate my spouse better. I won't feel so helpless when I disagree, and I will be better able to handle disagreements.

Disputing Question # 4: What bad can happen, or what bad can I easily make happen, if I keep my Belief?

E (Effective New Belief): If I keep my irrational Belief, I will feel out of control when I have an argument, I may feel helpless when I disagree, and my marriage may worsen.

It's easy to think an irrational Belief is true until you examine it closely, and looking for evidence is a good way to do this. Disputing is a scientific method that examines a Belief by searching for evidence to support it. In DIBs we ask, "Where is the evidence?"

What is evidence? Evidence is something other than your thinking, emotions, and behavior which suggests that your Belief reflects reality. You can detect evidence with your senses. For instance, you may believe it is raining outside; you can then look outside to see if it is raining. Your observation shows you if there is evidence for your Belief. If you see rain, you can keep your Belief. If you see no rain, you can give it up.

Some people believe that if they feel their belief is true, then it is true, but this is not the case. The emotion is created by the belief, so it is evidence the belief exists, but not that it is true. You may think, "I must do well on my final examination," and feel anxious, but the feeling of anxiety does not prove your Belief to be true. You may think, "I need a drink," and feel compelled to have a drink, but the compelling feeling does not prove an absolute necessity to drink. No, to find evidence, go beyond your feelings to your senses.

Conclusion

The ABCs and Disputing Irrational Beliefs (DIBs) are two of the most important techniques used in REBT. You can use the ABCs to discover your irrational Beliefs and use DIBs to eliminate them. These two techniques are simple but powerful, and can form a basis for comprehensive self-help with far-reaching change in your thinking, emotions, and behaviors. The ABCs lead you to discover your Beliefs about matters that are important to you—usually your behavior, the behavior of others, and the conditions of the world. DIBs helps you determine whether or not your Beliefs have an actual basis in reality. When you discover that a Belief has no basis in reality, you can give it up, along with the problems and misery it creates. By using these two techniques, you can work to eliminate the irrational thinking that makes it difficult for you to quit drinking (using), and this is good. By using them further, you may eliminate irrational thinking that affects you in many other aspects of your life which can help you in your recovery. Eventually, you may reach a point where you disturb yourself hardly at all.

8

You Can Quit: Eliminating Self-Defeating Beliefs About Quitting

Many people want to quit drinking (using). Some try and succeed; some fail. Unfortunately, many who fail end up drinking (using) more than they did before they tried to quit and failed.

Even though you have tried and failed, Rational Emotive Behavior Therapy (REBT) may help you succeed. By using REBT techniques, you can weaken and even eliminate the irrational Beliefs that make quitting so difficult while focusing on the rational Beliefs that help you attain your goal of sobriety. For instance, when you believe you *cannot* quit—you won't. It's that simple! When you give up that belief, you may do better.

The ABCs of Quitting

If you have failed to quit, you may upset yourself at the thought of the difficulties of quitting, and then drink more. In this chapter, we will Dispute several related irrational Beliefs which can create feelings of hopelessness. As you may recall, in Chapter 7 we presented the ABC model and we Disputed irrational Beliefs. The ABCs give you a clear picture of your upset and Disputing your irrational Beliefs helps eliminate your self-defeating Beliefs along with your self-defeating emotions and behaviors. In this chapter we will present examples of Disputes to help you give up your irrational Beliefs about being unable to quit.

If you have tried to quit and failed, do the ABCs to discover your irrational Beliefs. This can help you discover your irrational thinking, which is the most easily changed part of your upset. Here is an example of the ABCs you may find helpful. First, here is A, the Activating event:

A *(Activating event):* You tried to quit and you failed.

Second, look for C. Think of how you responded to your failure and ask, "How do I feel when I think of my failure?" In this example, let's say you feel depressed, hopeless and have feelings of self-pity.

To discover your bC, your *behavioral Consequence,* ask yourself, "When I think of failing, how do I act?" By doing this, let's say you discover the bC is that you hesitate to try again.

Now look for your B or *Beliefs* about the A by asking yourself, "What am I telling myself about quitting that gives me feelings of hopelessness, depression, and self-pity and also leads me to hesitate to try again?" You may discover the irrational Belief, "Because I have failed so often in the past, I'm a weak, defective person who can't quit; I can't stand failing again."

Disputing Irrational Beliefs About Quitting

Once you have completed the ABCs, the next step is using DIBs (Disputing Irrational Beliefs) to rid yourself of your irrational Beliefs about quitting. The following is an example of a Dispute:

iB (irrational Belief): Because I have failed so often in the past, I am a weak, defective person who can't quit; my failure proves that I will always fail.

D (Dispute): Is there any evidence that my Belief is true?

E (Effective New Belief): No! I can prove that I didn't quit. But, my past failures do not prove that I am so weak and defective that I absolutely *cannot* quit. I can prove that I failed, but I cannot prove that I will always fail.

D: Is there any evidence that my Belief is false?

E: Yes! Many people falter, and then pull through, even though they have disappointed themselves before. Therefore, I can too. Failing to do what I want does not make me a weak or defective person. My failures do not define my character or my essence, and they do not measure my ability to change or improve. They only reflect my present human fallibility.

D: What good can happen, or what good can I make happen, if I give up my irrational Belief?

E: Several good things can happen. I won't believe that I am incurably defective. Instead, I can merely accept that I am fallible. Then, I can believe it is possible to quit, and that gives me hope.

D: What bad can happen, or what bad can I easily make happen, if I keep my irrational Belief?

E: I may continue to fail, feel bad about myself, feel hopeless and depressed, and I will probably continue to drink (use).

The above example of DIBs shows how you can diminish your hopelessness about quitting by Disputing (challenging) an irrational Belief. Remember, you can feel a Belief is true, and you can act as if it were true, but your feelings and your actions do not prove it. They merely reflect the existence of a strong Belief. For instance, you can have a strong Belief that quitting is impossible. You can feel that it is true, and you can act as if it is true. However, this is not evidence that it really is true. Close examination by Disputing shows no evidence to support it. Through this process, you can see that your Belief is irrational, i.e., it leads to self-defeating emotions and behavior.

Now that you have an idea of how we use DIBs in eradicating Beliefs creating hopelessness at quitting, we can go on to other examples. Below is a Dispute concerning the Belief that failure proves an irreversible lack of will power.

iB: My failure to quit proves that I absolutely do not have enough will power to succeed, and that I can never quit.

D: Is there any evidence my Belief is true?

E: No! I can prove I didn't quit, but this doesn't prove I can't quit. I can prove that I did not have enough will power, but this still doesn't prove I will never have enough will power. Finally, there is no law in the universe that states I can never quit.

D: Is there any evidence that my Belief is false?

E: Yes! First, there is no evidence my biological make-up prevents me from succeeding, and there is no evidence my tendencies to fail are permanently fixed. Second, failing many times does not mean I must always fail. Without a doubt, other seriously addicted people struggled and failed before they made it. Yet, they did make it. The one thing that almost assures failure is for me to quit trying. Because I can keep trying, I may succeed.

D: What good can happen, or what good can I make happen, if I give up my irrational Belief?

E: I will have more hope so I can try harder and longer. When I falter, I will have less of a tendency to give up. Even though I have failed many times, I can keep trying.

D: What bad can happen, or what bad can I easily make happen, if I keep my irrational Belief?

E: I will easily give up trying. I will easily put myself down and feel guilty and ashamed, and I may continue giving myself problems with drinking.

Here is a Dispute of a Belief that you must go back to drinking once you have quit.

iB: If I quit, I'll have to go back to the good feelings I had when drinking (using).

D: Is there any evidence that my Belief is true?

E: No! I may want to go back to the good feelings, but there's no evidence that I have to. I may think that I won't like living without those good times (the high), but there's no evidence that I can't live without them.

D: Is there any evidence that my Belief is false?

E: Yes! First, I have engaged in many pleasant activities that I have stopped doing, and drinking (using) is just another pleasant activity—so I won't have to repeat it either. Also, before I ever had those good times, I survived and found some happiness, and I can survive and achieve happiness again. As well, many other people have survived without those good times, and some have discovered so much happiness without drinking that they don't ever drink again. So I too can resist going back.

D: What good can happen, or what good can I make happen, if I give up my Belief?

E: I may realize those good times are not as good as they once were, and I can imagine myself quitting without feeling desperate. Also, even if my past drinking was very good, I can steadfastly say good-bye to those past good times and stubbornly work at thinking about new and different good times.

D: What bad can happen, or what bad can I easily make happen, if I keep my Belief?

E: First, I may never quit. Second, if I keep my irrational Belief, I may quit, but I will feel depressed at being deprived, so I may easily relapse. Last of all, it would be practically impossible to appreciate the good life I can have without drinking.

We have disputed three irrational Beliefs that can lead to failure in quitting. Here is another. This one is the Belief that quitting must be easy before you can do it.

iB: Quitting should be easy; if it isn't, I can't do it.

D: Prove it!

E: I can't prove it! I want it to be easy, but wanting does not prove it has to be. I can prove that I haven't quit because I believed it should be easy, but I cannot prove that it truly should be easy before I can quit. Finally, I cannot prove that I absolutely can't quit.

D: Is there any evidence that my Belief is false?

E: Yes! It is obvious that quitting is not easy because many people struggle with quitting. If it should be easy, it would be and none of us would be struggling. Difficult doesn't equal impossible—it only means hard and no more, so effort is required to deal with it. Others have succeeded with difficulty, therefore, I can too.

D: What good things can happen to me, or what good things can I make happen, if I give up my Belief?

E: I can think of the joy of success instead of overly focusing on the struggles of quitting, and I can have hope that I can endure the challenges of quitting until I succeed. I will feel better knowing that part of the problem is my irrational Belief that I can't change. When I change my Belief, I will have more hope of doing better.

D: What bad can happen, or what bad can I easily make happen, if I keep my Belief?

E: I may give up trying. If I continue to try, I may feel miserable. Then I may drink to cope with my misery—and I may never quit.

In the above Disputes, we have examined several irrational Beliefs, all pertaining to the Belief, "I can't quit," and we found no evidence to prove them true. When you find your Beliefs have no evidence, it is easier to give them up. This does not guarantee you success, because success depends on other factors such as commitment and sustained effort. However, giving up the Belief that you can't quit gets you one step closer. It leaves you with a better way of thinking, as well as with one less irrational Belief to hinder you.

Remember, because you are human, you can easily go back to your flawed thinking. That is, once you have weakened an irrational Belief with Disputing, you can regain it by merely neglecting to work at eliminating it. So, creating lasting changes requires work and practice.

In summary, the examples provided are guidelines to help you learn the technique of DIBs. Once you learn this technique, you can Dispute the irrational Beliefs you find in your own thinking. To find these irrational Beliefs, use the ABC model to focus on your thinking when you are upset—and pay close attention! Once you discover these irrational Beliefs, you can work to eliminate them by using DIBs. You can find your irrational Beliefs are not supported by evidence, giving you more freedom to follow through with your rational thinking and rational behavior.

Rational Self-Statements

Rational Self-Statements are rational Beliefs that can help you attain your goals. Those listed below are specifically designed to help you quit drinking. After reading the list, select those that help you. Then, repeat them again and again—silently or out loud—until you feel a noticeable change in your emotions:

I can quit.

Quitting is not easy, but I can do it!

Quitting does not have to be quick and easy.

Quitting may give me frustrations, but I can stand them.

Other people withstood these frustrations and so can I.

Quitting is hard, but it's not too hard.

Drinking isn't the only fun in life, and I can pursue other forms of happiness.

I can live without the good times I have had.

I have tried and failed, but failing does not mean I am permanently weak and defective.

Failing does not mean I will always fail.

After I fail, I can forgive myself and continue to try.

Conclusion

We have now completed the discussion on eliminating the irrational Belief, "I cannot quit." By giving up this Belief, you can have a greater ability to follow through when trying to quit. It is important to remember, however, that even though the information in this chapter may give you hope, you can easily revert to your old way of thinking and believe that you cannot quit. This is normal.

So, what can you do to help yourself when you go back to your old ways of thinking? The keys are work and practice! By continuing to use the techniques and do the exercises in this chapter, you can strengthen your rational thinking so that you rarely, if ever, think you cannot quit drinking.

9

Eliminating Your Excuses for Drinking

Once people discover their drinking is a mistake, they often put themselves down, feel worthless and shamed, and believe that their feelings are too much to bear; yet they continue to drink (use). How do they continue even though they feel so miserable? One method is simple: they make up excuses and just keep on drinking (using). This, as Rational Emotive Behavior Therapy notes, is part of our fallible human nature, and it's normal.

If this is normal, what's the problem? Simply that you continue to suffer all the problems that using alcohol or drugs give you. You temporarily sidetrack yourself from your long term goals, and you continue to feel lousy. It's normal, but it's self defeating.

How do you create these excuses? First, you may sensibly think, "I am lousing up my life, and that is bad." Then you may crookedly think, "I'm a louse for failing; I'm worthless and I can't stand it; I have to drink to get rid of these feelings; all my friends do it, so it's no big deal." Or, you may tell yourself, "It's too hard to change; oh well, there's no use trying." In this way, you make yourself upset, then cover up your upsets and, at the same time, avoid the serious doubts that you have about yourself, your drinking, and your unhappiness—for a short while. You may even be killing yourself with booze while telling yourself that drinking is more helpful than not. If, however, you examine your thinking carefully, you can see that your excuses do not make sense, and that they prevent you from facing reality.

By eliminating your excuses, you abandon some of the irrational Beliefs that led you to continue your habit—and that is good. In this chapter, you'll see some of the common excuses people use to justify their drinking, together with rational responses which demonstrate the nonsense of this type of self-talk.

Rational Responses to Commonly Used Excuses

As you read each of the following excuses and their corresponding rational responses, look for the nonsense in them. These examples can help you see how you have deceived yourself. In this way, you can do better at recognizing your own excuses, rationalizations, and denials.

When you notice yourself making excuses about drinking or using, face it; you are merely using them to cover your upsets and your doubts about your drinking. Let's look at some typical excuses so you can unravel your nonsense thinking:

Excuse # 1: I am not really addicted.

Rational Response: Look at the way you handle alcohol (drugs). If you recognize a number of your beliefs and behaviors in the following list, face it—you have addicted yourself:

● Drinking (using) is your primary form of pleasure.

● You sometimes drink (use) to avoid problems.

● You have tried to control your drinking (drug use) and failed.

● You hate yourself for failing to control your drinking (drug use).

● You have tried to quit and failed, thinking it was too difficult.

● You believe you can't quit and you continue to drink (use).

● Often, you think you have to drink (use).

● You believe you harm yourself by drinking (using)—yet, you continue to drink (use).

- You upset yourself at your failure to quit and you drink (use) even more.

- You make excuses for failing to quit.

- After quitting, you feel extremely fearful of relapsing.

Excuse # 2: It's my nature to be addicted—it's in my genes.

Rational Response: It may be easier for you to addict yourself if you have the pre-disposing genes, but there is no law in the universe that states that you must follow the tendencies your genes give you or that you do better when you follow them. On the contrary, most recovered people find sober living to be easier and better. Have you ever heard a recovered person say, "I like what you're doing to yourself with drinking and drugs. The way you're living your life looks so wonderful that I'm going back to that old lifestyle to be just like you"? I haven't. If it's in your genes, so what? You can live better sober (clean).

Excuse # 3: I am special (or better than others), so I can be addicted without it hurting me; I can get away with it.

Rational Response: It makes no sense to regard yourself as better than others and insulated from the harmful consequences of addiction. Face it. These harmful results affect you. Instead of comparing yourself with others, compare your addicted self with your non-addicted self. Which you—the addicted you or the non-addicted you—can live longer and attain more happiness? Which you—answer honestly—will create more misery, live with excuses, and suffer more harmful consequences in the long run?

Excuse # 4: It's the only pleasure I have; life would be too boring without it.

Rational Response: Come on! It may be the only pleasure you have now, but is it the only pleasure you can ever have? Surely you can think of activities to enjoy without drinking. Thinking of other activities and following through by doing them takes effort, but it's worth it! Truly, many recovered people have found happiness without drinking, and they acknowledge that the happiness they attained is good. Furthermore, they know that they gained more by quitting than by continuing to drink.

Excuse # 5: *Other people make me drink (use); if they didn't give me so many hassles, I wouldn't have to drink (use).*

Rational Response: Pure hogwash! You and you alone are responsible for your drinking (drug use). You are the one who picks up the bottle, puts it to your lips and drinks! Quit using your anger at others as an excuse; quit drinking (using). Eliminate your anger and get a life!

Excuse # 6: *I'll wait until it's easier before I quit.*

Rational Response: Unfortunately, it may not become easier to quit, but it can easily become more difficult. At times, you may think it's easier—after a hangover or an alcohol-related accident— but you can quickly forget about quitting once the crisis is over. And the longer you continue drinking (using), the more likely it is that you will believe you need alcohol (drugs) and that you can't live without it. Give up this excuse and realize that the easiest time to quit is now!

Excuse # 7: *Everybody deserves one small vice.*

Rational Response: A vice is a self-defeating practice. Do you really believe that you deserve something that hurts you? Further, if you are unable to control this small vice, will you be able to prevent it from becoming a larger vice? You'd do well to give it up now.

Excuse # 8: Everybody needs an escape; this is mine.

Rational Response: People who often escape their problems and responsibilities think crookedly and do worse. Usually, they encounter a difficulty and tell themselves it's too hard and they can't take it. Then they head for something less demanding—like a bar. Yes, drinking can relieve immediate stress, but your emotional problems may remain or become worse as a result of continued drinking. Further, escaping your problems temporarily can contribute to long-term problems, including economic and personal crises. People may want to escape stress and responsibilities, but this doesn't prove a need to escape—it only proves that people are irrational! Come on! Nobody *needs* an escape! Get rid of this nonsense!

Excuse # 9: I didn't get arrested for drunk driving because I was drunk. I was arrested because I drove past a police officer.

Rational Response: When people are arrested for driving under the influence, if they are chronic drinkers, they rarely admit that drinking was the main cause of their arrest. Instead, they attribute it to other factors. They make excuses with such nonsense as, "The cop nabbed me to meet his quota," or "Can you believe my luck—the cop was right there when I made a wrong turn, and I just happened to be drinking!" If you were arrested for driving under the influence, unless it was truly a mistake on the part of law enforcement, you were arrested because you drank and you drove.

Excuse # 10: I don't drink for the effect of alcohol—I just drink a lot because I like the taste.

Rational Response: Then how did you get arrested for being drunk, and why do you drink to the point that it gives you problems? Yes, you may like the taste, but do you like the bad consequences of drinking? Is the taste worth it? Think about it! If you thought about the consequences while you were enjoying the taste, would you enjoy your drink as much? Hey, if you merely like the taste, then go out and buy yourself some non-alcoholic beer! If you won't do this, then stop trying to fool yourself and others—you like the high that you get from drinking, and you believe that you can't quit, or that it's too hard, or that you can't stand life without it!

Excuse # 11: Drinking may give me problems, but, oh well, it really doesn't matter.

Rational Response: This excuse is just another cop-out! When you tell yourself it doesn't matter, face it, it does matter. Why tell yourself such nonsense? Because you know you are harming yourself by continuing to drink, and you are upset about the problems related to your drinking. But, instead of facing these problems and managing them, you tell yourself this bull and hide your head in the sand with a bottle!

Why not? It's much easier for you that way, isn't it? For the short term—maybe. But in the long run your stress will still be there, along with the other problems related to your drinking, including hangovers, hassles from your spouse, and hassles on the job. Your best bet would be to manage your problems, beginning with your drinking. Sure, it's not easy, but, in the long run, quitting and remaining sober sure beats the hell out of all the hassles and problems you have to endure right now because of your drinking!

Excuse # 12: I can quit any time I want.

Rational Response: Can you do anything simply because you want to do it? Of course not! Wanting does not equal the ability to do what you want. However, by working at it, you can usually increase your ability to attain your wants. When you find yourself saying, "I can quit any time I want," don't use this statement as an excuse to drink. Instead, use it as an opportunity to recognize that you want to quit, and keep working at it until you do!

If you are telling this to others, you also may be telling yourself that you are no damn good because you can't quit or that it is too hard for you to quit. In either case, this kind of irrational thinking is a characteristic of addiction. If you can quit any time you want, then prove it to yourself! Begin right now and work at quitting and remaining sober! Others have, and so can you!

Conclusion

These are just a few of the common excuses people use to justify their continued drinking (using). Most likely, you have similar ones and many more! No matter how creative you get in making up excuses, they are about 99% hogwash, and you would be wise to get rid of them.

Recognize the fact that when you make excuses you have appropriate concerns and doubts about continuing to drink (use), and your excuses, rationalizations, and denials cover up your concerns. Once you are aware of this, you can begin to work to resolve the problems you see. The first step is to quit drinking! And refer to this chapter for help if you find yourself relapsing or even thinking that you might.

10

How to Stop Putting Yourself Down and Start Accepting Yourself

You like heavy drinking (using drugs) and you do it, but not without cost. Sooner or later you may do worse on the job, in your marriage, and with your children, and you may feel miserable. You may notice that other people have fewer problems, and that you could do better, but you make excuses and continue your drinking (using). You may compound these real-life problems with mental and emotional problems including feelings of worthlessness and low self-esteem. Self-downing, which creates these feelings, is among the most common self-defeating acts—and people who are having problems with drinking or drugging commonly do it. When you put yourself down, you can easily damn yourself for your mistakes, making it more difficult to correct them and making you feel miserable. Then, you may drink to manage your misery. By diminishing and even eliminating your self-ratings and by working to enhance your self-acceptance, you can develop a philosophy about yourself which will help you feel less miserable and more able.

Self-Rating vs. Self-Acceptance

When you rate yourself, you think in terms of your worth as a human being, and you tend to act accordingly. You may tell yourself, "I'm no damn good because I can't control my drinking —I'm worthless, so why try?"

You act according to your beliefs by working to prove yourself correct—acting just like a worthless human being (if one existed). On the other hand, when you accept yourself, you think, "I exist as a fallible human being. Yet, I want happiness, and I will work to get it." By accepting your fallible nature, you do not damn yourself for your mistakes. Instead, you rate your mistaken behavior as bad, and then you work to change it.

When you rate yourself, you also create feelings of self-esteem, both high and low. According to Rational Emotive Behavior Therapy (REBT), both are emotional disturbances, sicknesses that can easily defeat you. The view of self-esteem in REBT may be unique in the field of psychotherapy. Nearly all therapists agree with this view concerning low self-esteem. However, they differ on the issue of high self-esteem. Most exalt its advantages, i.e., it feels good, and it usually helps people do better than low self-esteem. However, we recognize that high self-esteem is a self-rating and has disadvantages. Because of this, and because you can do better by simply accepting yourself, we recommend that you stop rating yourself, thereby eliminating both high and low self-esteem. Then you can work to accept yourself and to strive for happiness instead of worth.

Forms of Self-Rating

Let's look now at several ways that people rate themselves, as well as how ratings influence their actions and behaviors. Once you recognize some of these problems in your thinking you can begin to work to eliminate them.

Self-Downing: Putting yourself down is one of the worst forms of self-rating. When you down yourself, you believe you are worthless. You feel lousy and depressed, and you tend to act the way you think and feel.

Self-downing often begins with musturbation about doing well. For example, you may think, "I must control my drinking, yet I am still drinking heavily; what a louse I am; I'm a failure and I can't stand failing; this is awful." Indeed, if you have no musts about yourself and your behavior, you will rarely damn yourself when you notice your mistakes or when others point them out to you. You will, instead, readily work to correct them.

Results of Self-Downing: What happens when you put yourself down? You easily create low self-esteem, depression, anxiety, shame, and guilt, along with ineffective behaviors such as shyness, laziness, and procrastination. You may:

- Think that you're a louse, a failure, and that you deserve to be punished.

- Believe that you can't do well, so you don't try hard.

- Avoid situations where you can make mistakes and avoid taking risks—no matter what the potential rewards.

- Deny that you make mistakes and make excuses for your behaviors.

- Fail to learn from your mistakes because you focus on your presumed state of lousiness rather than on your mistakes and how to do better.

- Believe that others know of your worthlessness and that they often reject you because of this.

- Drink to cope with your feelings of worthlessness.

- Drink while believing that you cannot attain a better form of happiness.

- Work to achieve worth instead of happiness.

- Align yourself with a strong leader [or religious or political entity—ed.] believing that you will gain worth by association.

High Self-Esteem: Elevating yourself creates high self-esteem or grandiosity. It is the opposite of putting yourself down. You have high self-esteem when you have thoughts such as, "I am a good person because I have done well," or "I am great because so many people admire me." People often ask, "Isn't it good for me to have high self-esteem, to feel good about myself?" In REBT, we think high self-esteem is better than low self-esteem, but not as good as self-acceptance, which is better than both. The following are some disadvantages of high self-esteem:

- You may believe you are immune from the harmful effects of alcohol or drugs (and other potentially harmful acts), thereby ignoring harm.

- You may not fully examine your mistakes, and you may think that you are so good that you can get away with them.

- When you succeed in attaining happiness, you may gloat in your feelings of greatness and quit working at what pleased you in the first place.

- You can believe that you are better than others and that you deserve more without doing more.

- You can easily neglect people or even do them harm because you believe that they are less worthy than you.

- You may overly criticize others, mainly because you like the good feeling of thinking that you are superior.

- Even though you do little that is admirable, you may believe others accept you merely because of your presumed greatness, and that they must approve of you even though you do little for them or even neglect them.

Rate Your Behavior and Not Yourself

When you rate yourself as either good or bad, your emphasis is more on you and your worth and less on the quality and effect of your *behavior*. You think mainly of yourself—either of your presumed worthlessness or your presumed superiority. Instead of rating yourself, you will do better to rate your behavior according to how well it helps you achieve your goals. Yes, it is good to acknowledge your successful behavior, as well as appreciate your talents and skills, such as you may have in writing, art, music, sports, socializing, sales, parenting, or homemaking. This is clearly not the same as rating yourself.

Errors in Thinking with Self-Rating

Self-rating, especially self-downing, is irrational because it easily sabotages your happiness and creates misery. With it, you feel anxious, guilty, ashamed, or grandiose, and you have either low or high self-esteem. You often fail to correct your mistakes, and you avoid difficult situations out of fear you will fail and prove yourself worthless. The following are some of the thinking errors involved in self-rating which show it to be irrational:

Over Generalization: When you rate yourself, you over generalize, i.e., you form a conclusion about yourself from a specific act. You may think, "Because I have acted good, I am good." First, you think rationally when you acknowledge your actions, but then you think irrationally when you believe you are the same as your actions.

To better understand, compare a specific act you did with a photograph of you. Both reflect a single event, yet neither represents all of you. No action or photograph ever could. Just as an unattractive photograph does not make you an unattractive person, a bad act does not make you a bad person.

Logical Fallacy: Sometimes self-ratings appear to be logical, but they can easily be shown to be false. For instance, in the morning you can do well and think you (the whole you) are okay. Then, that afternoon, you can do badly and believe you (the whole you) are no good. In the afternoon, you may even conclude that you were fooling yourself by thinking you were okay in the morning.

Does that make sense? If you think you are no good for your bad acts, why wouldn't you think you are good for your good acts?

All-or-Nothing Thinking: Rating yourself as a person who is good or bad is all-or-nothing thinking. You may rate yourself as all good or all bad, yet your actions are rarely all good or all bad. This type of self-rating can also contribute to your evaluating your behavior incorrectly. When you believe that you are a bad person, you can easily believe that your actions are all bad, when they are not. When you believe that you are a good person, you can easily think that your actions are all good, when they are not.

Accurately Rating Yourself May Be Impossible

By what measure can we accurately rate behavior? Is one behavior twice as good as another, and can one behavior be half as good as the next? To have an accurate rating, wouldn't you need a perfect criterion of goodness, as well as a perfect person to rate you—one who has complete knowledge of all your acts? Who could this person be? Would he be a Grand Rater on whom you would depend solely for all your ratings? Who would that be? Is it you? Is it your neighbor? Just who is it?

John, a hypothetical person, illustrates our point about rating people according to their behavior. Let us follow him throughout a day.

John arrived at work on time, greeted his boss warmly, procrastinated at starting a major work project, but he began working on it—and he performed fairly well. Then, he did exceptionally well on a minor task. Later, though, he had a three-martini lunch, stumbled and broke his nose. In the emergency room he saw a young physician who was pleased to see him because he wanted to work on broken noses. Then, John went home, took his pain pills, and enjoyed a movie on TV. Because of his injury, he missed a half day's work.

Now, considering his behavior, is John a good person or a bad person? Do you like John? How do you rate him? Were his acts all good or all bad, or do they fall somewhere in between? Who can give the final and correct rating of John—and according to what scale? Again, in REBT, we believe that rating people by specific actions does not accurately reflect the whole person. None of John's behavior reflects the whole John. This illustration shows how a person can act imperfectly, yet still succeed at some things.

Our main point is this: rating yourself is a serious error in thinking that can severely defeat you. Ratings that can help are ratings of your thoughts, emotions, and actions—about how they help or hinder you in achieving your goals.

DIBs: Eliminating Self-Ratings

You can see from the discussion above that we believe that rating hinders you, and you may begin to agree after reading our discussion. But how do you eliminate your self-rating tendencies? Disputing is a good start. It is the most effective way to demonstrate to yourself whether your beliefs in your own worthlessness or superiority have a basis in reality. Frequent disputing will go much further in helping you give them up such Beliefs. Here are several examples of Disputes:

iB (irrational Belief): Because I have failed, I am a failure.

D (Dispute): Is there any evidence to support my Belief?

E (Effective New Belief): No! I can prove that I've failed, but I can't prove that my failures make me a failure. A failing act doesn't equal failure as a person.

D: Is there any evidence that my Belief is false?

E: Yes! This Belief may be false because if I were a failure, I could never have done anything right and I would never be happy, yet I have done some things right and I have attained some happiness.

D: What good can happen, or what good can I make happen, if I give up my Belief?

E: I can stop feeling so depressed and self-hating, and I can have more hope of doing better at anything I may want to do.

D: What bad things can happen, or what bad things can I easily make happen, if I keep my Belief?

E: I will continue to hate myself for my mistakes and do worse at my attempts at doing better.

iB: I should be able to control my drinking like others; because I haven't, I'm no good; I can't stand it because I cannot control my drinking; it's awful.

D: Is there any evidence that my Belief is true?

E: No! No law of the universe says that I should control my drinking or that I am no good if I don't. I can prove it is bad to lose control, but not awful. And I can prove I do not like losing control, but I cannot prove I can't stand it.

This Belief may be false because if I had to control my drinking I would control it. Other people do not control their drinking, and this indirectly shows I don't have to control mine. If I were truly no good because of my lack of control, I could not do anything right. Because I have done some things right, I cannot be no good. And every time I have lost control, I have survived, which proves I can stand it.

If I give up my Belief, I may realize that I may not presently have the ability to drink as I want to, so I'd better give it up. And if I keep my Belief I will continue to fight this battle of trying to control my drinking while hating myself for failure.

iB: Because I have addicted myself, I am no good, a failure, and I deserve to be punished.

D: Is there any evidence that my Belief is true?

E: No! There is none! No law of the universe says that I'm no good or that I'm a failure, or that I should be punished. I can see that my doing a bad act, or many bad acts, shows that I am fallible, but it does not show that I am a no-good, worthless human being.

This Belief may be false because other people have addicted themselves, and they are not bad people. Also, I have done some things well: I have achieved some happiness for myself, and I have pleased others, so I cannot truly be a bad person.

If I give up this Belief, I can have more hope that I can help myself. I can admit that I have addicted myself without feeling miserable. I can think of my addictive behavior as it truly is—a serious problem, yet one that does not warrant my damnation or punishment.

On the other hand, if I keep my Belief, when I think of addicting myself, I will hate myself, make myself anxious when I think of quitting, feel guilty when I think of the harm I have done to others, and struggle harder to quit. Worse, I may give up on the idea of quitting altogether.

Besides Disputing irrational Beliefs to eliminate low self-esteem, you can also Dispute irrational Beliefs that create high self-esteem. Here is a DIBs for high self-esteem:

iB: Because I can drink so much, I am great.

D: Is there any evidence that my Belief is true?

E: No! I can prove that I can drink a lot, but I cannot prove that I am great. My Belief may be false because even though I can drink more than others, I still do harm to myself and sometimes to others. If I keep this Belief, I can fail to seek happiness from other activities. I can believe that I am above others and that they should admire me, and I may become incensed at people who criticize me for drinking. I will do better to acknowledge my drinking for the consequences it can give me—it might give me more pleasure than it will give someone who doesn't drink as much, but it might kill me sooner and give me more trouble than I would have if I didn't drink.

Do You Have Worth?

People often ask, "If I cannot be worthless when I do badly, and if I am not a better person when I do well, do I have worth?" In REBT, we believe people do not have absolute worth. You can think you have worth, and you may then feel worthy, but neither thoughts nor feelings prove the existence of worth. However, you do have worth to yourself because you can achieve happiness for yourself, and others can have worth to you because you can enjoy them.

What is the practical implication of our view? You will do better to stop chasing feelings of worthiness and get on with solving your problems and seeking happiness. When you quit rating yourself, you can do this much easier.

How to Gain Self-Acceptance

Accepting yourself, we think, is much better than rating yourself. By accepting yourself, you acknowledge both your mistakes and your successes, and you continue to work toward the goals that give you happiness. By eliminating your self ratings, you minimize misery and save precious time spent ranting and raving. The following is a discussion of self-acceptance and examples of how you can do better by accepting yourself instead of rating yourself:

Self-Acceptance: A general philosophy of self-acceptance is, "I exist, and I want to continue my existence; I want happiness, and I will work to attain it." When you accept yourself, you clearly think of your actions and rate them in terms of how well they help you. These rational Beliefs not only help you to feel helpfully frustrated at your mistakes, they also allow you to learn from them. Overall, when you accept yourself, you think in terms of your desires for survival and happiness. You think about your behavior and how it can help you attain these goals. As you seek health and happiness, you view mistakes as errors to acknowledge and to correct. If you relapse, you can think, "I did bad and that is bad, and I want to do better—so I'll keep trying! Now, how did I fail, and how can I change?" Then, you can work at changing.

Work For Happiness: When you accept yourself, how do you act? You acknowledge that you want happiness and that you will work to accomplish it. Because heavy drinking can shorten your life and give you more problems than many other forms of pursuing happiness, you may want to stop so that you will live longer and achieve more happiness. Then, your primary good feeling will be happiness, not self-worth or a drug-related high. You will think more of how to enjoy yourself instead of how to raise your self-esteem; and you will learn more about what you enjoy without drinking, and then you will seek that enjoyment.

React to Your Helpful Bad Feelings: With self-acceptance, you can feel appropriately bad when you are disappointed, because that can help you. Helpful bad feelings—such as annoyance, sadness, and regret—merely feel bad, but not miserable. On the other hand, hindering bad feelings—such as anger, depression, and guilt—feel miserable.

With self-acceptance, you can react in self-helping ways when you feel appropriately bad. For example, if you feel sad, you can think of what you can do either to change your circumstances or to accept them. When you can't change them, you will move on to other activities. Likewise, you can more easily quit drinking simply because drinking gives you hassles and not the catastrophes that you presume. You do not have to make yourself severely depressed or guilt-ridden to know that something is wrong, and you do not have to "hit bottom" to quit drinking.

Fully Admit Your Mistakes to Yourself and Work to Change: With self-acceptance, you will fully admit your mistakes to yourself without rating yourself and without developing self-hatred and low self-esteem. What is a mistake? There are two kinds: trying and failing, and failing to try. After admitting either of these mistakes, you can look closely at it and examine the specific thoughts, emotions, and actions that led you to make it. Then, think of what you can do in the future that may enable you to attain what you want. To help, use the REMAC technique (Rational-Emotive Mistake Analysis and Correction) to analyze your mistake and rate your bad behavior. The following is an example of REMAC:

My Goal (What I Want to Do): Quit drinking.

How I Acted: Last night I got drunk.

Rating My Behavior But Not Myself: I did badly. I got drunk and that wasn't what I set out to do. My behavior was lousy, but that doesn't mean I am a louse.

Thinking of My Mistake: How did I start drinking? What thoughts, emotions, and actions did I experience that led me to drink? Specifically, what irrational Beliefs defeated me?

Thinking of a Better Approach: What rational Beliefs will help me? How can I change? What steps can I take that might work better at helping me quit drinking?

Acknowledge Your Successes and Work To Continue: When you accept yourself, you fully acknowledge your successes. Tell yourself, "I did well—it's good." Doing this gives you an appropriate good feeling about doing well, and the feeling helps you notice your success. On the other hand, if you think you are basically no good, you may not notice that your success is the result of your own actions. Instead, you may think it is due to luck. Yes, luck can help. But even if you get a lucky break, you don't accomplish much unless you follow through.

When you do well, remember the steps you took and keep working. You can think, "I did okay. Now, how did I do it? What Beliefs led me to do it? What behaviors made it happen? How can I do that again?"

Try, Try Again: When you accept yourself, you may fail repeatedly, but you keep trying. If you are trying to quit drinking and if you are failing, your failure to quit does not prove that you have a character defect requiring God's intervention to change (as AA teaches). It's a failure in your thinking, feeling, and actions. Forgive yourself so that you can learn from your mistakes instead of dwelling on them. Then keep trying.

Rational Self-Statements

Rational Self-Statements are rational Beliefs designed to help you achieve your goals. You can select the ones you like or devise some new ones of your own. Repeat them until you feel better and make plans to act accordingly. Then, remember them so you can use them when you upset yourself.

When I do badly, it doesn't make me bad.

Although I have failed many times, I can still do better.

I have hurt and neglected others—but I am not worthless.

I exist, and I want to continue to exist. I like happiness, and I will work to get it.

If I do well, I am not great—I am just happier.

No matter how much I dislike my bad acts, I can still accept my fallible self.

If I fail in the future, it will be bad, but I will not be worthless.

Even though I have not done well in the past, I can attain happiness.

Conclusion

In REBT, we believe no one is a worthless human being. We make mistakes because of our fallible human nature. It is also in our nature to think irrationally and put ourselves down for our mistakes, as well as to elevate ourselves when we succeed. However, in REBT we believe that you will do well to fully acknowledge and correct your mistakes. Further, it is wise to acknowledge that you can do better if you stop rating yourself, no matter how often you fail and no matter how well you succeed. There is no reason that you must do well or that you are a louse if you don't. Even though you do not like making mistakes, you can stand making them, and you can reflect on them, learn from them, and then make changes. By steadfastly accepting yourself and rating only your behavior, you can focus less on yourself and concentrate more on changing the inappropriate behavior that defeats you. With this new outlook, you can begin to work toward your goal of happiness.

11

How to Have Less Misery When Quitting

Thinking of giving up something you've done for a long time can be difficult, like losing an old friend. Sometimes, you may even think life without booze wouldn't be worth it. However, you also know that drinking gives you problems—hangovers, conflicts at work and with family—and maybe even trouble with the law! And the misery can seem far worse than the problems. However intense the misery of giving up alcohol may feel, it is created by your irrational thinking and not by abstinence itself. Yes! An irrational Belief that you create (and that you can eliminate) creates your misery. In this chapter, we will show you how to recognize them and how to work to get rid of the Beliefs that create the misery of doing without.

Low Frustration Tolerance Related to Doing Without

When you think of quitting, you think of giving up something that you like, and this is rational. However, you may also recognize that your drinking gives you problems, so you have better reasons to give it up than to continue. Yet, you still keep drinking. Why? One reason is that you may think that you should be able to quit without discomfort and that remaining sober is awful. You may think that quitting is just too hard, and that you can't stand not drinking. This irrational thinking creates Low Frustration Tolerance (LFT), a form of misery that can make the difficulties of abstinence seem worse than your problems with drinking.

Low Frustration Tolerance (which we also call Discomfort

Anxiety) is an upset at the conditions of daily living—usually some form of discomfort or difficulty. You may believe that you can't stand the feelings you get when you don't drink (use), or that you enjoy getting high too much to give it up. These irrational Beliefs exaggerate the bad feelings of doing without to the point that you may become intolerant of even the thought of quitting, and thus give yourself feelings of depression and despair.

Give up the Beliefs *awful, can't stand,* and *too hard* if you think that it's bad to do without, but that it's also bad to keep drinking. If you give up those Beliefs, you will gain a more realistic picture of both drinking (using) and quitting. And it will be easier to appreciate which is better for you.

DIBs for Eliminating the Misery of Abstinence

To eliminate your upsets about doing without, you can Dispute the irrational Beliefs that create your LFT. Start by doing the ABCs. Your A can be doing without drinking (drugs) and the activities that go with it. Your C can be boredom, depression, or some other form of gloom and pessimism. Your B can be, "I shouldn't have to feel uncomfortable; I can't stand it; it's awful."

Now, let's look at the examples. The following three Disputes can help you rid yourself of the irrational thinking that creates LFT related to abstinence:

iB (irrational Belief): I must not feel bad; I can't stand the feelings I get when I think of doing without; it's awful.

D (Dispute): Is there any evidence that my Belief is true?

E (Effective New Belief): No! I don't like the feelings I have, but there is no reason that I must not have them. Disliking them is easier than not standing them, and facing my bad feelings is difficult, but not awful.

D: Is there any evidence that my Belief is false?

E: Yes! Even though I do not like these feelings, I have been able to stand them. Besides, other people have tolerated them, and so can I!

D: What good can happen, or what good can I make happen, if I give up my Belief?

E: If I give up my Belief, I can feel less miserable, and I can look forward to quitting with hope and less stress. Although it may be difficult to face my feelings, I can tolerate them and quit drinking (using) more easily.

D: What bad can happen, or what bad can I easily make happen, if I keep my Belief?

E: If I keep my Belief, I will feel miserable and helpless, and I may conclude that quitting will always lead to unbearable grief.

iB: I must have the good times that alcohol (using) gives me; I can't stand to give up the good times; it would be awful.

D: Prove it!

E: I can't prove it. What's more, this Belief may be false because I have done without the good times in the past, so I probably can do without them in the future. If I give up this Belief, good things can actually happen: I may eliminate the misery of doing without and realize there are more pleasant things to do than drink. I can work more on long range plans and enjoy them more—I may even have better good times than I had with drinking. If I continue to have this Belief, I may be in serious trouble: I may continue to feel miserable and depressed and I may never give up drinking.

iB: I can't stand not drinking with my buddies; it would be awful not to see them as I have in the past.

D: Is there any evidence that my Belief is true?

E: No! There is no evidence to support my Belief! Of course I can stand not drinking with my buddies. I will not like it for awhile, until I find other things to do, but I can stand it. Besides, I did well before I met my drinking buddies, so I can eventually do well if I decide not to see them again.

The following DIBs can help you in eliminating LFT about boredom:

iB: I can't tolerate the boredom I will have if I quit; it's too much to bear.

D: Is there any evidence that my Belief is true?

E: No! I have tolerated boredom before, perhaps only for a short time, but I did tolerate it. Also, other people who quit manage to tolerate it without serious problems, and many develop interests that keep them active and pleased with their lives. And, after I quit, I will have more money—not to mention a clearer head—with which to find ways to enjoy myself. I could easily end up less bored that I am now!

The following are three DIBs that can help you eliminate LFT creating pessimism about quitting and remaining sober:

iB: If I keep wanting to drink (use), I can't remain sober (clean).

D: Where is the evidence?

E: There is no evidence! I can want to drink (use) without doing it. The desire will not last forever, and I can think of the harm drinking causes me—which I do not want; and I can think of the happiness I can have with abstinence—which I do want.

iB: Booze is too hard to resist.

D: Prove it!

E: I can't prove it! There is no evidence that it's too hard to resist. There's evidence that it's hard, but not too hard!

iB: I can't function without alcohol.

D: Is there any evidence that this is true?

E: No! This is all-or-nothing thinking. I do function without alcohol—perhaps not as well, but I do function. Even if I don't do as well, I can work at doing better. And, almost certainly, if I quit drinking and stay straight, sooner or later—probably sooner—I'll end up functioning better than I do now!

Discover Your Own Irrational Beliefs and Dispute Them

After considering the problems that Low Frustration Tolerance (LFT) may give you when thinking of abstinence, you would be wise to discover your own Beliefs creating LFT. Even if you have quit drinking, you may still hold on to some of these irrational Beliefs. If you do, remember to do the ABCs. Think hard about your thinking. You may discover Beliefs such as, "I can't stand living without drinking," or "I shouldn't have to feel uncomfortable." Then, Dispute these Beliefs. By Disputing your irrational Beliefs about doing without drinking, including those about withdrawal symptoms and the loss of friends, you can see the nonsense in these Beliefs. Once you get rid of this type of thinking, doing without booze will not seem to be nearly as bad. You will feel better about quitting and have more hope for happiness. If, however, you keep your irrational Beliefs, you may create misery for yourself, including depression, despair, and hopelessness.

Good Results from Disputing

Several good things may happen to you when you diminish your LFT about abstinence and the misery of doing without. They include:

- Quitting and remaining abstinent will become easier.

- You will feel less desperate when you think of living without alcohol, and you may have fewer urges and thoughts about drinking after you quit.

- When thinking of the benefits of quitting, you can appreciate them more. For instance, when you think of living longer, with an increased ability to enjoy life with fewer hassles, it is easier to recognize that these benefits can be yours. However, if you are still telling yourself, "It's awful to live without drinking," these benefits will not seem as possible to achieve.

Common Questions About Abstinence

During discussions of abstinence, people often ask, "Do all people have frequent cravings when they quit?" The answer is No. Some people say that quitting was the easiest thing they ever did. Deciding to quit was difficult, but abstinence itself was not. Eventually, they have some cravings, but when they resist them they don't become severe problems.

People also frequently ask, "Do those who remain sober ever quit thinking of drinking?" The answer is that people who have quit sometimes have thoughts about drinking, but those thoughts do not always create problems. As well, the frequency of such thoughts tends to decrease with time (after quitting). Still, it is realistic to believe that you will have thoughts about drinking occasionally and to believe that you can tolerate it when you do.

Some people have few problems with unwanted thoughts about alcohol. Remember Craig (from the Preface)? He experienced a three-month period of extreme hardship without thinking of drinking until someone asked him how he could go though it all without drinking. He simply did not think about it!

Managing Your Boredom

One of the problems quitting creates is that you have a great deal of time on your hands, and you may find little to do. Well, challenge yourself to think of new activities and do them—take action! Even if you only *think* that you might like an activity—give it a try! Here are several ways of dealing with boredom:

- Think of activities that you enjoy more than boredom. Right now, you may not be able to think of anything more pleasant than drinking (using), but you can think of something more pleasant than boredom, can't you? Think! Try organizing a recovery meeting, writing, painting, working out, wood-working, playing golf or tennis—do something you enjoy!

• The most important thing you can do in the long run is to think of a long-term goal you want to accomplish, such as finding a better job, a mate, or an absorbing hobby. This can be difficult if most of your pastimes have been easy pleasures such as drinking or using, but you can do it. Another option is to absorb yourself more in enjoyable long-term activities that you are presently doing. Then, start working to accomplish your goals! Chapter 17 on happiness can help with this.

• Plan—*NOW!* Make a definite plan to pursue some new activities. Take deliberate steps to put your plan into action. At the first opportunity—today or tomorrow—put your plan to work and make it an action plan!

Rational Self-Statements

You can try the following Rational Self-Statements. These are Beliefs that can help you cope and work toward happiness. You can repeat them to yourself several times to determine which seem most suitable for you. Usually, they work better after Disputing because you are then thinking more rationally.

I can quit; I can look forward to a better life; and I can withstand any hardship.

I can stand living without drinking (using).

It may feel bad to do without, but only bad, not awful. In the long run, I can enjoy myself more by doing without booze (drugs).

When I whine about quitting, I make quitting worse.

It's hard to live without booze (the high), but it's also hard to live with it.

If I quit drinking (using) and work at long-term happiness, I'll do better instead of worse.

If I don't have a good high from alcohol (drugs), so what! It's no big deal!

I'll think more of the benefits of abstinence and the hardships of drinking (using).

Conclusion

It is important to recognize the nature of your stress when you believe you cannot tolerate the misery of doing without booze or drugs. So, what is it? It is your hindering emotions which can include Low Frustration Tolerance, depression, despair and boredom that are created by absolutistic thinking, i.e., your *musts, can't stands,* and *awfuls.*

You can overcome these miserable feelings. You can Dispute your irrational Beliefs to show yourself that they are nonsense and that you do not have to feel miserable when abstinent. Work to replace the pleasurable feelings you have with drinking (using) with pleasurable feelings and activities you may gain in sobriety. It is wise to remember that the difficulties you can have with abstinence are usually small compared to the problems created by heavy drinking, even though it does not always feel this way. Eliminate this addiction and start enjoying activities you can do without so many hassles.

12

Eliminating Misery and Stress Without Drinking (Using)

As you know, drinking and drugging yield some benefits. They help you loosen up and forget your troubles—at least for a while. From the beginning of civilization (or since the discovery of the fermented grape), drinking and drugging have been a common method of escaping life's difficulties. However, overall, they do poorly at helping you handle tension and stress. They easily sidetrack you from facing and resolving your problems. They may also create serious mental and physical problems.

You can learn to deal with stress without drinking (using). Rational Emotive Behavior Therapy has techniques that work well for many people. When you apply them, you may diminish or even eliminate your stress, and you may go even further. You may hardly ever make yourself disturbed again. A large order? Yes, but still possible. Let's see how.

Stress (Secondary Upsets) and Drinking (Using) to Cope

You are human and humans feel stress at times. It's part of our nature. If you don't deal with it, you can easily increase your difficulties. Booze (drugs) may relieve stress for a short time, but it doesn't help in the long run. Eventually drinking (using) can cause you more stress and problems.

What is stress? It is usually an upset at an upset. As first mentioned in Chapter 6, we call this a Secondary Upset. For instance, you may feel depressed. Then, you can make yourself depressed at your depression by telling yourself, "I shouldn't be depressed; I can't stand it; it's awful." Depression is your Primary Upset and thinking you should not be depressed is your Secondary Upset.

Let's take it one step further. Say you find yourself tense and pressured and telling yourself you need a drink (hit) to cope with stress. Telling yourself you need a drink is a Tertiary (Third) Upset. You don't have to drink to deal with stress.

Mary illustrates another way of dealing with stress: using the ABCs of REBT and Disputing Irrational Beliefs (DIBs). Mary had been abstinent for several years. She hadn't contemplated drinking until her recent divorce. Then, her ex-husband sold their house without her permission, and she was upset about it. She presented her problem at one of our training sessions for group leaders. We helped her do the following ABCs to identify her irrational Beliefs. Here is what we found:

Primary Upset

A (Activating Event): My ex-husband sold our house without my permission.

iB (irrational Belief): He should not have sold the house.

iC (inappropriate Consequent emotion/behavior): Anger.

Secondary Upset

A2 (Secondary A): The Primary Upset (above).

iB2 (Secondary iB): I can't take feeling so miserable.

iC2 (Secondary iC): Low Frustration Tolerance, depression, impulsive action.

Drinking to Cope

A3 (Tertiary A): The Secondary Upset (above).

iB3 (Tertiary iB): I need a drink to deal with this stress.

iC3 (Tertiary iC): More stress.

Mary had already decided that she did not need to drink, but she wasn't doing well because she hadn't dealt with the other upsets. We first helped her Dispute her Secondary Upset, (iB2) which was "I can't stand this stress," then her Primary Upset (iB), which was "He should not have sold the house!" By Disputing, she realized that she could handle the stress. She also realized that there was no reason her ex-husband should have acted differently than he did. Even though his behavior was bad, it was not awful. She said, "I can take this stress, and I can see there is no reason he should do what I want. It was bad that he sold the house, and I don't like it one bit, but I can't do anything about it now. So, I'll accept it."

Our recommendation to Mary was to go further in eliminating her irrational thinking by continuing to Dispute her irrational Beliefs. Then, she could more fully acknowledge the problem without disturbing herself, as well as do what she could to resolve the remaining problems with her ex-husband and the sale of the house. It was bad that her husband sold their house without her permission, and she would do well to accept it and try to manage the problems it caused.

What happened to Mary when she continued to work on her upsets using the techniques and advice we gave? She attained good results. She no longer felt compelled to drink, she didn't feel miserable, and she handled the problems that were created by her ex-husband's actions. By identifying and Disputing her irrational thinking step by step, she successfully managed her stressful situation without drinking.

Again, how did Mary work out her problem? First, with the group, she worked on her last upset first, then her Secondary Upset, and finally her Primary Upset. Why eliminate upsets in that order? Because upsetting yourself about an Activating event (A) easily prevents you from taking corrective action. When the Activating event is your own upset (a Primary Upset), you will not do well at working on it until you eliminate your upset about having it, your Secondary Upset. We recommend Disputing the irrational Beliefs (iBs) creating your last upset—whether it is a Tertiary Upset (I need a drink), or a Secondary Upset (I can't take this stress). In Mary's case, "I need a drink," would come first. By realizing that she didn't need a drink, she could then Dispute the notion that she couldn't stand the stress. Finally, she worked on her Primary upset, which was her Belief that her ex-husband shouldn't have sold the house. After Disputing, which helped her think more rationally, we then offered practical advice, because people can use advice better when they are thinking rationally.

Bob, a client of mine, is another illustration of how the ABCs and DIBs can help someone handle stress without drinking. Bob worked as a foreman in an electronics and communications firm. Much of the time he could not do his job properly because the owner would not spend enough money on equipment, services, and personnel. Bob said he needed to drink every night to unwind from work. He drank heavily on weekends as well. After a few weeks in counseling, Bob realized his drinking was also a problem. I suggested he do the ABCs, and this is what he found:

Primary Upset

A: There is too little time and not enough equipment for me to do the job well.

iB: I must do well.

iC: Anxiety, guilt, tension.

Secondary Upset

A2: The Primary Upset (above)

iB2: I can't stand this; I need to feel better.

iC2: Low Frustration Tolerance, depression, impulsive actions.

Drinking to Cope

A3: The Secondary Upset.

iB3: I need a drink to unwind.

iC3: Drinking.

How did he quit? After doing the ABCs and discovering his activating event and upsets, he experimented with his drinking and he kept track of his tension at work. When he felt tense, sometimes he drank and sometimes he didn't. When he drank, he found that he didn't feel any better. He felt worse instead. He also handled his problems worse when he drank. He forgot his problems for a while, but they were still there in the morning. His conclusion? He decided that he didn't need a drink to manage his stress. In fact, he decided that drinking didn't help him at all with his problems; instead, it created more problems. He concluded that quitting was the best solution.

To help with his decision to quit drinking, he used the DIBs technique first to dispute his Tertiary Upset, then his Secondary, and finally his Primary Upset. He did the following:

Disputing the Tertiary Upset (Drinking to Cope)

Disputing Question: Prove that I need a drink to unwind! Is there any evidence?

Effective New Belief: I can't! There is none! I want a drink, but that does not prove I need one.

Disputing the Secondary Upset

Disputing Question: Where is the evidence that I can't take feeling stressed?

Effective New Belief: I can't find any! Other people have dealt with stress, and I can too.

Disputing the Primary Upset

Disputing Question: Where is the evidence that I have to do well?

Effective New Belief: Nowhere! I may want to do well, but that does not prove that I have to. Other people have had to deal with problems like mine, and they did not have to do well either.

Disputing Question: Can I prove that doing well gives me worth?

Effective New Belief: I can't prove it! Doing well may give me happiness, but it does not give me worth.

What were the results? First, Bob felt less miserable and he no longer felt tense and anxious. Next, because of his discontent with the way the company was managed, he considered looking for another job. However, after weighing the advantages and disadvantages, he decided to keep his present job and look for other ways to manage the problems at work. He also discovered that he had been a workaholic and had neglected to take vacation days, thinking he had to stay on the job to keep things running. Now he realized the company wouldn't fold without him and he decided to take his vacations regularly. Remaining sober and resolving his work-related stress gave him the added benefit of a happier home life. He came home from work instead of stopping off at a bar; he was more relaxed at home and enjoyed his family more, and his wife was pleased with his change.

Using DIBs to Eliminate Stress Without Drinking

Can you eliminate your stress like Bob and Mary? There's a good chance that you can when you use the techniques that they used. You may not do perfectly well with these techniques, but you can work with them until you learn to do better with them. Eventually, you may eliminate your stress almost completely and hardly ever upset yourself again. Then, your emotions will serve you better, especially when you no longer use them as an excuse to get bombed.

Why use DIBs to deal with stress instead of using booze or drugs? Let's compare them. Drinking (using) offers you an escape from stress. DIBs, on the other hand, offers you an elimination of stress. Drinking (using) is easier, but it often takes up a lot of your time, and you can feel bad afterwards. DIBs, on the other hand, is harder, but you can do it in a few minutes, and you can feel relieved afterwards. Finally, drinking, in the long run, can give you health problems and more stress on top of your day-to-day problems. DIBs, in the long run, may eliminate your stress completely.

In Chapter 7, we Disputed the irrational Belief, "I need a drink." Here are more examples of DIBs for Secondary Upsets:

Primary Upset

A (Activating Event): You are working on a sales presentation before seeing your potential customer, and you are thinking about how important it is to obtain the customer's business.

iB (irrational Belief): I must do well during my presentation; it would be awful to fail; I can't stand it if I do not win this contract.

iC (inappropriate Consequent emotions): Anxiety, tension.

Secondary Upset

A2 (Activating Event): The above Primary Upset.

iB2 (Secondary irrational Belief): I must not feel tense and anxious; it's awful to feel this way; I can't stand it.

iC2 (Secondary inappropriate Consequent emotions): Anxiety, tension.

Dispute of Secondary Upset

Disputing Question #1: Prove it! Where is the evidence that I must not feel tense and anxious; that it's awful to feel this way; and that I can't stand it?

Effective New Belief About Upsets: I can't prove it! I do not like feeling tense and anxious, but there is no law in the universe that says that I must not have these feelings. I can prove that it is bad, but not awful, and I can prove that I do not like these feelings, but not that I can't stand them.

Disputing Question #2: Is there any evidence my Belief is false?

Effective New Belief: Yes! Many people get tense and anxious before trying to make a sale, and they stand it. I am human, so I too can stand it. It is bad that I am upset, but not awful, and no law in the universe says that I must not upset myself.

Disputing Question #3: What good can happen, or what good can I make happen, if I give up my Belief?

Effective New Belief: If I give up my Belief, I can feel better: I will eliminate the tension created by these Beliefs, and then I can work to eliminate my Primary Upset so I can feel even better. Also, I can prepare more efficiently. Even if I do well at eliminating my irrational thinking and, yet, do not get this contract, I will be more prepared to eliminate my worry and anxiety about the next presentation. I will have fewer urges to drink, so I will have fewer thoughts about drinking to distract me.

Disputing Question #4: What bad can happen, or what bad can I easily make happen, if I keep my Belief?

Effective New Belief: If I keep my Belief, I may remain miserable about my tension. I may think a lot about drinking and I may even drink. I will have no more ability to deal with my emotions the next time I talk with a client.

iB2: I can't take feeling depressed.

Disputing Question: Is there any evidence that I can't take feeling depressed?

Effective New Belief: No there isn't. I don't like feeling depressed, but there is no law in the universe that says I must not feel it or that I cannot take it. If I don't tolerate feeling depressed, I will not be able to understand how I upset myself and how I can eliminate it. Then, I will easily make myself depressed many more times in the future. Because I do not like feeling depressed, I will do better when I realistically believe I can take it. Then, I can think about how I create my depression, and I can work persistently to eliminate it.

Rational Self-Statements

Besides using DIBs, you can also use Rational Self-Statements. When you find yourself upset at an upset, use the following Rational Self-Statement to help you accept that you are human and that you are going to upset yourself at times. Tell yourself:

It's human to get upset, so I will probably upset myself repeatedly.

Most people upset themselves some of the time.

Because I am human, I think crookedly.

I can accept myself even though I upset myself.

Being disturbed does not make me worthless.

Conclusion

To achieve the best results for eliminating your misery and stress—quit drinking! You don't need it! Then, deal with your stress by facing it and not by escaping it with booze or other drugs.

It is human nature to upset yourself and to create feelings of stress about your circumstances. Unless you make an effort to change, you will continue to upset yourself. To eliminate the irrational Beliefs that create your stress, use the information in this chapter. It works! It's not easy—it takes work and practice—but the results are worth it! Others have succeeded; so can you!

Now, we have completed our discussion about the different problems that you can create for yourself when you drink heavily, as well as why people drink and how to quit. In the following chapters (through Chapter 17), we will focus on problems and upsets of everyday living, including anxiety, anger, depression, and Low Frustration Tolerance. All of these can be a part of your drinking problem, and they often contribute to relapse. So, after quitting, working on these problems is an important part of continuing your recovery and working toward a better life.

13

Eliminating Anxiety and Guilt About Doing Well

Many people want to do well in their achievements—in work, in school or in their hobbies—whatever they consider important. However, when you go beyond wanting to do well to believing you must do well, you can easily create anxiety and guilt. These keep you from accepting yourself, especially your mistake-making nature. Eliminating them is wise if you want to succeed and to enjoy yourself while doing so.

Anxiety and guilt are common. When you create these upsets, look first for Secondary Upsets—your misery about your misery—and work to eliminate them.

Gary, a businessman and a former client of mine, provides a good illustration. He had been clean for some time. In one of his counseling sessions, he stated he was worrying about receiving a large contract. The contract could be very lucrative—several million dollars, in fact—and he had an appointment to meet with his potential financier. He found himself obsessing about the meeting, which hindered his preparing for it. His concentration was poor, and he was losing sleep.

First, we discussed his thoughts about his worrying, his Secondary Upset. He thought that because he had been in this business a long time and had done this before, he shouldn't be worried.

"Where's the evidence that you shouldn't be worried?" I asked. "Yes, you have done this before, and you know what you are doing, but that doesn't mean you absolutely should not worry about it, does it?"

"I see your point," he said.

He quickly saw that he was upset about his upset, and that it didn't make sense to think he shouldn't worry. Then, after he began to accept that he can upset himself, we went on deal with his Primary Upset, his worrying.

What made him worry? He believed that he must come out of this meeting with a contract.

Simply *wanting* the contract would make him feel concerned, which would be rational and self-helping. However, believing that he *must* have the contract created anxiety, which clearly hindered him.

Gary's irrational Belief was, "I've got to come out of that meeting with a contract." Once he began Disputing this Belief, he realized it was irrational. By Disputing the Belief every day for several days, he was able to get rid of his anxiety before he met with his potential financier. Although he did not obtain the contract, he did go on to be successful in his business because he was able to successfully apply the DIBs technique to other upsets.

Many people assume Gary's worry was normal and wonder why we consider it to be irrational. "Are you saying something is wrong with me when I worry?" they ask. Yes! Of course something is wrong! An upset, as we view it in REBT, is to think, feel, and act in a way that defeats you; we do not consider an upset to be okay merely because it is normal. Think about it! Worry, which is normal, feels lousy and holds you back. Do you want that?

A good analogy to this is the common cold. Every year most people catch a cold or the flu, and this is normal. But, they don't want it. It is the same with upsets. Emotional upsets like anxiety and guilt are common human failings that people do not want. It's unwise to disregard them just because they are normal. You'll do better to accept your upsets as being self-defeating and then to work at eliminating them.

Just what do you do to yourself when you feel anxious and guilty? First, you want to do well, and this is rational. Then you think you must do well, and this is irrational and self-defeating. Along with your lousy feelings of anxiety and guilt, you overly focus on yourself and away from your goals. You think that you must do well, that you are no good if you fail, that you can't bear failure, and that your mistakes are awful.

This we call your ego. You create your ego when you demand perfection of yourself and when you rate yourself. You can eliminate these perfectionistic demands by understanding how self-defeating they are and by ridding yourself of the Beliefs that create them. By giving up the Beliefs that create your ego, you eliminate your anxiety, guilt, and low self-esteem, and you quit overly focusing on yourself as well. You can then concentrate more on accomplishing your long-term goals.

Beliefs That Create Anxiety and Guilt

Anxiety and guilt are upsets about you, and you create them with musts about doing well either in your accomplishments or in your social relationships. You create anxiety with thoughts such as, "I must have control and make events turn out well," or "I must do well in important matters or else I am no good; it's awful to fail; I can't stand doing less than perfectly well." To create guilt, you have thoughts such as, "I must not hurt others, but I did and I am no good for doing it."

Disputing Irrational Beliefs About Doing Well

How can you eliminate your upsets about your mistakes and failings? Let's say that you've been making yourself anxious or guilty. First, complete the ABCs to identify the perfectionistic Beliefs that you hold about yourself. The next step is to work at eliminating them. When you successfully eliminate them, you will then feel concerned about failing and you can think more of how to succeed, which in turn will allow you to accomplish more.

In REBT, after doing the ABCs, we have found that Disputing is the next step because it does well in eliminating emotional disturbance for most people. After you have worked with DIBs, you can try other techniques. The following are examples of using DIBs to eliminate anxiety. If you find yourself experiencing these kinds of emotional upsets, the next examples may help you Dispute your own irrational Beliefs. First, let's look at the DIBs for an irrational Belief that creates anxiety about drinking and relapse.

iB (irrational Belief): I must not drink; I must stay sober; if I fail, I'm no good; it would be awful to relapse; I couldn't stand to fail again.

D (Disputing Question): Is there any evidence my Belief is true?

E (Effective New Belief): No! There is evidence that my drinking is a poor way to deal with stress and that it harms me, but this is not evidence that I must not drink! Also, there is evidence that I will make a mistake if I drink, but none that I am no good if I do. Finally, I can prove that I would not like to fail again, but I cannot prove that I can't stand it.

D: Is there any evidence that my Belief is false?

E: Yes! I drank in the past, and I may drink in the future. I want to remain sober, but that doesn't mean I absolutely have to. I have failed in the past without becoming a failure or a no good person. When I failed, it was bad but not awful. Also, I drank in the past and I stood it, so I may stand it now and in the future.

D: What good can happen, or what good can I make happen, if I give up my Belief?

E: I can accept myself as a human being who can make mistakes, and I will stop worrying myself sick about relapsing. When I fail, I will be less inclined to make excuses and to be hard on myself. Instead, I will think clearly of my mistake and how to prevent it from happening again. I can think more easily of the reasons I want to remain sober and not of my presumed lousehood if I fail. Then, I will feel helpfully concerned about relapse, but not miserably fearful.

D: What bad can happen, or what bad can I easily make happen, if I keep my Belief?

E: I may upset myself about the problem of staying sober. If I drink, I may hate myself and damn myself severely. I may drink to diminish my misery and make excuses for relapsing. This can prevent me from thinking clearly about how I relapsed and how I can become abstinent again.

The above Dispute can help you when you make yourself upset about drinking and relapse. The next DIBs can help when you are overly concerned (anxious) about doing well at any particular task or accomplishment:

iB: I must do well or else I am a failure; I can't stand doing less than perfectly well; it's awful to do badly.

D: Is there any evidence that my Belief is true?

E: No, there isn't! I can find evidence that I want to do well, but none that I have to. I can prove that I failed, but not that I am a failure. I can prove that it is bad to make mistakes, but not that it is awful. I can prove I do not like doing badly, but I cannot prove that I can't stand it.

To challenge this belief even further, my belief may be false because if I must not fail, then I cannot fail, yet sometimes I do. Also, other people make mistakes without becoming failures; so can I. Finally, even though it is bad to make mistakes, and I do not like making them, I have been able to stand it.

If I give up my belief I can live better with myself, even when I disappoint myself. I can work to enjoy myself and not to prove myself. I can think more of how to accomplish my goals instead of the presumed horrors if I don't. When I think of failure, I will suffer less and accomplish more.

On the other hand, if I keep my Belief, I may continue to demand that I do well, and this will keep me worried and anxious. I will do less and enjoy myself less because I will overly focus on failure—which I presume to be horrible. This may contribute to more failure.

Next is a DIBs for eliminating irrational thinking that creates guilt:

iB: I must not neglect, hurt, or offend others; it is awful if I do, and it makes me a louse; I can't stand it when I do something that disappoints or offends others.

D: Is there any evidence my Belief is true?

E: No! There is no evidence! Even though I don't want to hurt others and I know that it's bad to do so, that doesn't mean that I must not offend others or that it is awful to do so. When I do hurt others, its a lousy act, but it doesn't make me a louse. And, even though I do not like disappointing others, I can stand it.

I can challenge my Belief even further by considering the fact that it may be false. The reason is that I have disappointed and neglected others in the past, but I did not become worthless, even though I may have thought that I was. Even though it was bad and I did not like it, I have been able to stand it.

If I give up my belief, I will find it easier to acknowledge my mistakes and to forgive myself when I hinder or disappoint others. I will find it easier to think clearly of what I did wrong and to learn how I may do better next time. And, I can enjoy myself with others instead of overly concerning myself about neglecting them.

If I keep my Belief, I can easily feel guilty about my mistakes. I will then think more of the presumed horror of making mistakes, making it more difficult to correct them. Then, I may withdraw from people to avoid feeling guilty, or I may overly apologize and be considered a nuisance.

Rational-Emotive Imagery for Anxiety and Guilt

By Disputing the above irrational Beliefs creating anxiety and guilt, you can begin to eliminate your self-sabotaging Beliefs. To help you further, you can do the following Rational-Emotive Imagery exercise:

First, imagine yourself in a situation where you believe you must do well or you should have done well, for instance, when performing at a sporting event, writing a paper for school, or talking with an important person. Then, imagine yourself doing a lousy job, even the worst you can imagine. Allow yourself to feel anxious or guilty. Hold that image and emotion for about a minute. Now, while you keep that image, change your emotion so that you are no longer upset. Repeat this exercise two or three times.

The following list provides examples of other situations in which people commonly disturb themselves about doing well. If you find yourself feeling anxious or guilty in situations such as these, consider doing a Rational-Emotive Imagery exercise to eliminate your upset:

- Performing in front of others, i.e., giving a speech or a theatrical performance.

- Seeing a very attractive person you would like to get to know.

- Talking to a salesperson about paying a fair price.

- Teaching your child to deal with a problem or to change a behavior.

- Disciplining your child and wanting it to work.

- Taking a test.

Accept Yourself as a Fallible Human Being

Humans are not created with the ability to succeed all the time. So, when you demand perfection of yourself and believe you must do well, you are setting yourself up for misery. Think about it. To do exactly as you want, you have to know your abilities perfectly well, know perfectly well the ins and outs of the task you are to perform, and then follow through perfectly. Imagine any task that you want to do and ask yourself if you can have the ability to accomplish it perfectly well. For instance, can you know everything there is to know about swinging a golf club, taking a test, or making a presentation before an audience? Hardly.

Instead of demanding perfection, what is a better way to approach your tasks or responsibilities? You can first accept that you are a fallible human. Then, set out to accomplish what you want while keeping your goal in mind. Next, focus on how you can achieve results, then make adjustments along the way, and continue until you accomplish your objective. If you do badly, so what! Keep trying! By letting go of the irrational Belief that you must do perfectly well, you can focus on working to attain your goals. By joining the fallible human race, you will no longer try to be superhuman—almost godlike—in your endeavors. Instead, you can focus on some form of happiness that is attainable, and you can keep working for it. That's not so bad, is it? We think you can achieve more happiness with this approach than by demanding perfection.

Work for Happiness Without Perfection

When you think realistically about the idea of perfection, it makes little sense to consider it a valid goal. Can you or anyone else perform a perfect act—where there is no flaw or error? Perhaps, but most likely not! Can you find perfection in anything you do? Again, the answer most likely is No! Professional golfers usually make mistakes during a round of golf, even when they win, and rarely do they make a hole in one. But they still enjoy the game, and they gain a great deal from playing the sport. You may know a friend or loved one who has plenty of faults, but you still care for that person. So you will do better to pursue your goals and to recognize that you can accomplish them, though not perfectly. When you think of accomplishing your goals, consider the following points:

● Think of happiness instead of superiority and perfection.

● Think more of doing than of doing well. How much happiness escapes you because you do too little? After drinking or drugging, aren't procrastination and goofing off the primary ways you neglect your happiness? Do more things instead of trying to do things more perfectly, and you will accomplish more and find more pleasure in what you do!

- Allow yourself to do mediocre work if it will give you more happiness. For instance, if you have a limited amount of time to work on three projects of almost equal importance, you may gain more from completing all in a mediocre fashion instead of completing only one very well.

- Work at improving your performance. Don't forget that you want to do well, and doing well usually requires practice. So prepare. Prepare for speeches, rehearse how you can meet an attractive person, and plan your next work assignment.

Rational Self-Statements

The following are Rational Self-Statements you can say to yourself to help you deal with your perfectionistic tendencies:

I will focus on doing and not on doing perfectly well.

I want to do well, but no law in the universe says that I must.

Nearly all my happiness occurs without perfection.

Persistence, not perfection, is the key to success and happiness.

When I think too much about mistakes, I make more of them.

When I fail, I can keep trying.

Conclusion

If you strive for perfection, you may realize more misery than happiness. Perfection is an illusive quest that creates anxiety and guilt. Doing poorly or badly doesn't make you less worthy, but it can disappoint you—for a short while at least. So when you make mistakes, work at accepting yourself, even when you fail badly. Remember—if you haven't done well yesterday or today, you still have tomorrow. Accept yourself even though you are fallible. Go ahead, begin now to work for happiness and not for perfection.

14

Facing Rejection Without Anxiety, Guilt, or Shame

People concern themselves about acceptance and rejection. Many, though, make themselves overly concerned. When you do so, you don't merely want approval so that you can have a relationship—you think that you absolutely *must* have it so that you can have worth. You may think, "I need approval—if I don't get it, I'm no good and that would be awful." This type of thinking is absolutistic and creates the self-sabotaging emotions of anxiety, guilt, and shame, as well as low self-esteem. Becoming aware of these Beliefs and eliminating them will allow you to get rid of many upsets and to attain more happiness with others.

The following illustrates this. Let's say a woman—we'll call her Sharon—is contemplating her first date with John. She feels excited while thinking of her attraction to him, of wanting John to like her, and of wanting him as a companion. Her thinking helps her because it gives her awareness of her preference. However, if she adds the irrational Beliefs, "I must have his approval or else I'm no good, and if I get rejected, it would be awful," her focus changes from anticipating the delight of John's acceptance and friendship (created by her rational Beliefs) to apprehension and anxiety (created by her irrational Beliefs). This is self-defeating because her feelings of anxiety can easily lead her to act shyly and nervously. Her shyness and nervousness may contribute to her being rejected, and that is just the opposite of what she wants.

Sharon's thinking can influence the outcome of her date. Let's look further at how this can happen. First, if Sharon thinks rationally, her goal is to enjoy herself with John. What would it take for her to enjoy herself? She would pay attention to him and to how she enjoys his company. She would express her opinions and act in ways enjoyable and agreeable to her. If she is thinking irrationally, however, she may do several things that can interfere with her enjoyment. If he makes a disagreeable statement, she may act as if she agrees, not giving him the opportunity to know her thoughts and feelings. She may also hesitate to let him know what she desires in their relationship or in the activities she wants to do because of fear of conflict and rejection.

This illustrates just one of many ways absolutistic thinking about either approval or rejection can defeat you. The following are a few other ways the fear of rejection can lead you to act inappropriately. You may:

- Choose activities mainly to get approval and not because you enjoy them.

- Worry about how well your friends like you instead of considering how well you like them.

- Have difficulty breaking away from relationships that you no longer want.

- Frequently look for signs of disapproval.

- Worry constantly about losing a friendship.

- Continually demand reassurance and acceptance from others.

- Drink because you believe it helps you attain the approval of others.

Using DIBs to Eliminate Your Dire Need for Approval

Having a dire need for approval gives you less happiness—not more—because you constantly focus on your fear of rejection which creates anxiety, guilt, and shame. It can also lead you to make a nuisance of yourself through constant demands for approval.

What can you do to overcome your dire need for approval? Start with Disputing your irrational Beliefs! Then continue with some of the other procedures in this chapter. The following are examples of some irrational Beliefs that can create anxiety about approval and rejection, and ways of Disputing them:

iB (irrational Belief): I must have approval from others or else I am worthless; it's awful to be rejected; I can't stand it when others don't like me.

D (Dispute): Is there any evidence that my Belief is true?

E (Effective New Belief): No! None! I may want approval, but that does not mean I must have it and that I am worthless if I don't get it. It's bad to be rejected, but I cannot prove it's awful. Finally, I can prove that I don't like rejection, but not that I can't stand it.

D: Is there any evidence that my Belief is false?

E: Yes! People have rejected me, and I did not become worthless. It was bad but not awful, and I survived. Rejection is not the end of the world. I can find happiness in other ways, and I may find someone else who will accept me. Also, I do not enjoy all people, so I can easily see that some people will not like me.

D: What good can happen, or what good can I make happen, if I give up my Belief?

E: I will feel less anxious and depressed, and I can think constructively instead of desperately about approval. I can enjoy myself more, especially when I am with others. And, when I think of activities I want to do, I'll be less concerned about what others think. I will then choose my activities because I like them and not for approval. All of this will give me more happiness.

D: What bad things can happen, or what bad things can I easily make happen, if I keep my Belief?

E: I will feel anxious when I am with others. I may follow the crowd instead of my own desires. I may crave love and affection, and yet I will hesitate to approach people and speak to them for fear of rejection—all resulting in less happiness for me.

iB: I must have love or else I am worthless; I can't stand being without love; it's awful.

D: Is there any evidence that my Belief is true?

E: No! I want love, but there's no reason I must have it. Even though having someone's love can be enjoyable, I have been without it, and I have found that I don't need love for my worth or for my survival. It's bad to be without love, but it's not terrible. Finally, in some ways, I can attain happiness better without having love. I can pursue more relationships; I can do more for others; and I can absorb myself in interesting hobbies. I'll do well to give up this Belief so I can do better at getting the love and enjoyable life that I want.

Look for Self-Downing: Identify the self-downing that may create your upsets about approval and rejection. Ask yourself, "Do I think rejection makes me worthless?" If the answer is Yes, you can Dispute your self-downing Beliefs. Consider the following Dispute:

iB: If I am rejected, or if I don't receive love, I am worthless and I don't deserve happiness.

D: Is there any evidence that my Belief is true?

E: No! I can find no evidence that rejection makes me worthless. People have rejected me, and I continued to have the potential for gaining happiness. If rejection makes people worthless, then nearly everyone would be worthless—but they are not. Also, if my Belief were true, it would help me, but it doesn't—it hurts me. Indeed, I can either keep my Belief and feel desperate, worried, and anxious, or I can give up my Belief and still want love and approval without feeling desperate.

Look for Awfuls, Horribles, and Terribles: Look for the *awfulizing* in your thinking. Ask yourself, "Is it *awful, horrible,* or *terrible* to receive rejection?" If the answer is Yes, then identify your irrational Beliefs and Dispute them. The following is an example of a Dispute of this irrational Belief:

iB: If others know of my mistakes, it's awful.

D: Where is the evidence?

E: Nowhere! If others know, sometimes it may be bad, but not awful, horrible, or terrible, and sometimes it may be good. For instance, some people will feel more comfortable with me when they know that I accept myself as fallible. And, some may even want to help me when they learn of my mistakes.

iB: It would be horrible to be rejected.

D: Prove it! Where is the evidence?

E: There is no evidence! Being rejected may be bad, but not horrible. It cannot be so bad that it is worse than bad. If I give up my Belief, I will realize that being rejected is not a nightmare but merely a problem.

Look for Can't Stands: Identify other absolutistic thinking you may have including *can't stands* if you are rejected or don't receive the approval that you want. Then, Dispute these Beliefs.

iB: I can't stand being rejected.

D: Is there any evidence that this is true?

E: Not one bit! But there's plenty of evidence that I can stand it: I have often withstood rejection, and others have withstood it too. By getting rid of my *can't stands*, I'll be less depressed because I'll think more appropriately about rejection—I won't overdo it, and I can think more about the fun I can have with people.

Disputing can quickly weaken an irrational Belief so that you can immediately do better in a situation where you create a dire need for approval. DIBs can also help you in overcoming most of your worries associated with approval and rejection. However, this takes work. So continue using DIBs until you develop a strong philosophical change—a change in the way you think and feel about approval so that you hardly ever upset yourself about it.

Other REBT Exercises and Techniques

In this section, we present other REBT techniques. Read through them and give them a try. DIBs and the Rational-Emotive Imagery exercise are usually the most helpful REBT techniques. The imagery exercise is the quickest to use—you can usually do it several times within ten minutes. However, be sure to try each one because they all can help. And remember, the more you work, the more rationally you will think, and that can lead to more happiness!

Rational-Emotive Imagery: To eliminate your irrational Belief, create an upset using Rational-Emotive Imagery and then work to eliminate it. Instead of feeling inappropriately anxious and desperate, you can feel appropriately concerned or sad. Do the following:

First, imagine that you are approaching someone, and that you want acceptance from this person. Then, imagine this same person rejecting you. With this image in mind, allow yourself to feel upset (perhaps self-pity or depression). After you have allowed yourself to feel these emotions for a minute or longer, change your upset to an appropriate emotion. Hold this emotion for another minute or so.

How did you change your emotions? By changing your thinking. You kept the same image but changed your thinking about it, and your emotions changed.

Here is another Rational-Emotive Imagery exercise: Imagine that you are finishing a work project and turning it in to your supervisor. Then imagine the worst—your supervisor looks it over, frowns, and throws it back growling, "This stinks—do it over, you idiot!" With this image in mind, allow yourself to feel upset. Then, after a minute or so, change your feelings to a helpful emotion. Hold this emotion for another minute. By doing this exercise, you can see that after you upset yourself, you can change your emotions so that you feel differently.

In REBT, we believe by doing this type of exercise you can train yourself to have appropriate emotions such as concern or sadness when you think you may be rejected instead of the hindering emotions of anxiety and depression. By repeating this exercise, you can strengthen your rational Beliefs and eventually have fewer upsets regarding approval and rejection.

Shame-Attacking Exercises: Shame is a disturbance people create by overly concerning themselves about the views other people have of them. For instance, you may worry others will find out about your mistakes, and believe that if they find out, they will think you are a despicable no-goodnik and this would be horrible.

To attack and weaken your feelings of shame, REBT recommends, in addition to Disputing and Rational-Emotive Imagery, that you try a behavioral shame-attacking exercise. You can deliberately create situations you believe will result in your getting rejected. Then, while in them, you can work at refusing to upset yourself. Of course, it is important to choose only situations that are harmless and that will not cause short or long-term problems for you or others. Here are some examples:

- Walk down the street—wearing your shirt backwards.

- Walk into a restaurant, and, before you are seated, politely ask for a free meal. Don't insist, but act sincere and considerate.

- Stand on a street corner under a street sign and ask passers-by, "I'm lost—can you tell me how to find (the name of the street on the sign)?"

- Stand in a large department store and shout out the time: "Ten forty-two and all's well!"

When you put yourself in such situations with this behavioral exercise, you may notice the rejection of other people. For instance, you may notice looks from people that convey, "you are really odd!" and you may get ushered out of the restaurant or the department store. In this way, you can experience the rejection that you previously imagined and you can see that it doesn't have the significance you thought it would—it isn't awful, horrible, or terrible, and it doesn't diminish your worth.

Sometimes people ask, "Are you saying it's okay to act badly so that people reject you?" No! The consequences tell you if an act is good or bad. In the shame-attacking exercise, you deliberately set things up so nothing bad happens, such as your getting arrested or physically harmed.

Another question people ask is, "If you say I don't need approval, then why concern myself about getting it?" Because approval is important when you want the cooperation of others. When you ask an attractive person for a date, you get the date only if you receive approval. When you want the date, you also want approval—so you will be wise to concern yourself about approval, but not to worry about it.

Approval and Drinking Self-Assessment: Another exercise you can do is to assess whether or not you drink (use) because it is what you want to do, or because you want the approval of your drinking (drugging) buddies. When you think of drinking (using) and you have problems with it, ask yourself if the acceptance of others has anything to do with your desire to drink or use. If it does, then you are exaggerating the importance of acceptance, as well as using alcohol (drugs) to provide a way to get the approval you seek. You will do well to eliminate your irrational thinking and enjoy the company of people who do not require you to do something you do not want to do—such as drink or use drugs. If you really don't want to drink (use), then don't! To help in your self-assessment, ask yourself the following questions. If your answer to these questions is Yes, work more at eliminating your irrational Beliefs about acceptance and rejection:

Am I thinking about drinking (using) because someone would approve if I drink?

Am I thinking that I must have acceptance and that drinking (using) will give it to me?

Do I drink (use) to comply with others' wishes?

Do I feel upset when others disapprove of my abstinence?

If you answered yes to any of these questions, you'd better consider your dire need for approval and how it badly affects you. It really is unwise to keep a bad habit merely because it gets the approval of others. There are other people who do not want you to harm yourself, and you'll do well to cultivate their friendship.

In-Vivo Rational Self-Statements: In-Vivo means "in life." For this exercise, in the presence of others, think the following Rational Self-Statements:

I want the approval of some people, but not all. I don't have to have anyone's approval.

I can't control these people, and I can't force them to like me.

If I get rejected, I am not a rotten person.

I'll look out for myself first, not them.

When you do this exercise, notice if your emotions change, and if they do change—how. Also, notice, after you feel better, if you quickly feel miserable again. This shows you how quickly you can go back to irrational thinking. Remember, it is human nature to revert back to former behavior. With more work, you may eventually eliminate it so that you hardly regress at all.

Work Toward a Rational Philosophy of Approval: You can work toward a rational philosophy of approval that includes some of the following Rational Self-Statements:

I want approval when it affects my happiness, but I do not have to have it.

It's good to have the approval of people who live and work with me.

If my actions lead to disapproval, it may be a unfortunate, but it's not a catastrophe—no matter how much people reject me, I am never damnable, and I can still try to act better the next time.

If I am rejected, I can still accept myself and work to have acceptance next time.

I don't like being rejected, but I can stand it.

Some people will never approve—no matter how well I do, and some people will like me even though I do badly.

Conclusion

When you find yourself worrying about approval or rejection, you will be wise to develop a rational philosophy that will help you relate well to the people who are important to your happiness while retaining your own ability to remain helpfully independent —not overly dependent on the wants and desires of others. Believing that you need approval is absolutistic and can easily hinder you from seeking the happiness that you want. It easily creates anxiety, guilt, shame, and low self-esteem. With these hindering emotions, your behavior is overly influenced by the preferences of others. For instance, if others like the color blue, you will too, or if they drink, you may drink to please them.

Remember, you do not have to have approval, and it won't give you worth. And—yes—you can stand rejection. Even though being rejected is bad, it is not awful. You do not have to worry about approval or feel devastated if you do not get it. Disappointed? Yes! Upset? No! So, when you are rejected, work to accept yourself no matter how miserably you have failed and no matter how bad your disappointment. Then, continue to seek the company of the people you enjoy.

15

How You Can Eliminate Your Anger

At times, people act in ways that you don't like, and you feel angry. Anger is a typical human emotion, but in most instances it hinders more than it helps. When you're angry, you think irrationally, which can lead you to act inappropriately. You may create problems for yourself, as well as for people in your line of fire. You may fear losing control and getting into trouble with others, and you may drink to control your emotions and behavior. Because of the problems created by anger, it's wise to eliminate it altogether.

Why Eliminate Anger?

You do worse when you are upset, and anger can result in severe, unwanted consequences. When angry, people easily make unfair demands, obsess about the wrongs of others, plot revenge, inappropriately rebel, or commit violent acts, including physical assaults, or worse—murder! Anger is created with thinking such as, "You must treat me nicely and act just as I want or else you are no damn good. I can't stand your bad behavior. It's awful, and when you act badly you should be punished." These beliefs can get you crazy enough to hurt people. Changing this type of thinking can help you get rid of the anger you have created. Then, with appropriate emotions, you can more easily handle the challenges of difficult people and situations.

That's right—you create your anger. As with all other irrational Beliefs, you can eliminate anger by disputing the absolutistic thinking that creates it. Then you can learn to feel appropriately annoyed instead of angry at the bad actions of others. Instead of ranting and raving, you can communicate your discontent in a sensible, constructive manner. You may go further; with the changes you make in your own behavior, you may begin to notice that people have positive as well as negative qualities.

How to Eliminate Anger

How can you eliminate your anger? First, it helps to understand that anger is created by your own irrational thinking and not by other people or events.

Many people believe others cause their anger. This is not the case. Other people do help you create your emotion: if they didn't act as they do, you wouldn't have an emotion in response. But you are responsible for the quality of your emotion, be it anger, annoyance, or indifference. For instance, you may believe you are angry because your spouse criticized you, or someone cut you off in traffic, or an employee arrived late for work. This is not the case. You are the one who chooses how you react emotionally. So step one in eliminating your anger is to take responsibility for it.

A common recommendation for eliminating anger is "Get it out —express it." This normally creates more anger—not less. When you practice doing anything, it doesn't make the behavior go away, instead it makes it easier for you to do it. This includes expressing your anger. So, "getting it out" merely helps you to make yourself more angry next time.

Yes, you may quickly feel relieved by forcefully expressing your feelings, but the people who are in your line of fire may feel alienated or become angry themselves. Secondly, exploding, even if no one is around, doesn't provide lasting relief and, again, can prevent you from learning how not to become angry. Therefore, in REBT, we believe that by dramatically expressing your anger you get short-term relief and long-term problems. On the other hand, you can get long-term relief by eliminating your anger and by continuing to feel annoyed, so you can react appropriately to bad situations. By recognizing the thinking problems you have in creating your anger, you can quickly begin motivating yourself to take responsibility for it and to work at eliminating it. Some common thinking problems created by anger are:

- Concentrating more on the other person's behavior than on your own.

- Fixing your attention on matters you don't like instead of on those you do like.

- Thinking in all-or-nothing terms and focusing on the bad in people, ignoring the good.

- Over generalizing by believing all people are hopelessly bad.

- Abandoning your job or marriage instead of managing problems related to another person's difficult behavior.

Next is a list of common, unwanted effects of anger. While reading the list you may recognize some of the results of your anger. This can motivate you to work to eliminate your upsets. As you read the list, ask yourself, "When I anger myself, do I:

- disrupt my relationships with others?

- increase my difficulties in resolving problems with others?

- inappropriately rebel, i.e., automatically act contrary to what others want?

- disrespect the rights of others to live as they choose?

- love someone, but let my anger lead me to treat them badly and drive them away?

- provoke others to become angry with me and reject me or act argumentatively with me?

- withdraw from others?

- want to drink to deal with my stress and feelings of alienation?

Disputing Absolutistic Thinking That Creates Anger

To eliminate your anger and the problems it creates, first identify your irrational thinking. Ask yourself, "When I get angry, what am I telling myself that creates my anger?"

Discover your irrational Beliefs and start working to eliminate them. The following DIBs can help you get rid of the absolutistic thinking which contributes to anger.

iB (irrational Belief): You (other people) must treat me nicely and kindly and in just the way I want; I can't stand it when you treat me badly; your behavior is awful; you are no damn good for treating me badly, and you should be punished.

D (Dispute): Is there any evidence that my Belief is true?

E (Effective New Belief): No! I can prove I do not like their behavior and that it's bad, but I cannot prove that they must not do it or that their behavior is worse than bad, i.e., awful. Also, I can prove they are fallible, and I can prove it would be good if they were held accountable for their acts, but I cannot prove they are no good and should be punished. Finally, I can prove I do not like their behavior, but I cannot prove I can't stand it.

D: Is there any evidence that my Belief is false?

E: Yes! Often people have treated me badly or unkindly, but I have always survived. Also, because some people have severe emotional problems, they may find it exceptionally hard not to treat people badly, including me. If they absolutely must not treat people badly, then it would be impossible for them to mistreat anyone—yet people do treat others badly. If they were bad, then they could do no good. Yet they do. Finally, punishment does little long-term good, and some people do worse when they receive punishment.

D: What good can happen, or what good can I make happen, if I give up my Belief?

E: I will feel better. I will feel only annoyed, so I can act rationally toward people who are treating me badly. I can react to others with tolerance while respecting the fact that they are fallible. I can treat others as I myself would like to be treated. When someone is acting extremely irrational, I can feel strongly annoyed and yet act appropriately. This way, I will be less inclined to commit an act that I will regret. My rational thinking and useful negative emotions will help me have fewer conflicts with others, and I will worry less about severe consequences, including arguments and fights. Also, this will help me develop lasting relationships with those who are important to me, and I will be able to manage extremely difficult people in such a manner that I do not create further problems for myself.

D: What bad can happen, or what bad can I easily make happen, if I keep my Belief?

E: I may remain angry and resentful, and this can easily lead me to treat others badly. If I emphasize their bad behavior, I will not see their good behavior, and I will have less understanding of them. This will lead me to make more mistakes. Then, I may act badly—driving away most people who know me and care for me. And, worse, if confronted with extremely difficult people, I may commit an act that could result in my being arrested or even imprisoned.

REBT's View of Punishment

Quite often people do not understand the belief we hold in REBT that it is irrational to think people who commit bad acts should be punished. It is not uncommon for people to ask, "Is REBT soft on people who commit crimes, including assault, murder, and rape, and do you suggest that it is good to coddle those who commit such crimes?"

Our answer is No! However, neither do we believe that punishment is a good approach. We believe that people usually create beneficial change when they see that a change is good. We believe that they will change primarily through education, training, and their own hard work, as suggested in this book, and not by working on a chain gang. We simply believe that punishment rarely creates lasting beneficial change. It may occasionally help to motivate people, but it is not a complete solution for society or for the person committing the crime.

Of course, when people repeatedly and seriously hurt others and do not respond favorably to psychological or medical help, we believe that penalization is warranted. But we also believe that simple removal from society can adequately prevent further disruption by the wrongdoer, and that additional punishment during incarceration is unwarranted and probably harmful.

Also, quite a few people ask, "Do therapists trained in REBT believe that all people are good?" No! We believe people do both good and bad acts, but are neither all good nor all bad.

DIBs About Government's Religious-Oriented Rehabilitation Programs

The following Dispute can be helpful to you if you've been required to attend AA or another religious program and recognize that it is not beneficial to you:

iB: The government should not require me to go to a religious-oriented rehabilitation program; it is awful to be forced to attend; I can't stand it; I must be given an option.

D: Prove it! Where is the evidence?

E: There is none! I can prove I do not like it, but I cannot prove that the government must not do it. I can prove it is bad, but not that it's awful; I know that I do not like it, but I cannot prove that I can't stand it. And, finally, although an option would be better for me in my rehabilitation, I do not have to be given an option.

I can challenge my belief further by considering that it may be false because many people are not given options in alcohol and drug treatment and are required to attend 12-step religious programs. These include people convicted of DUIs and people who are imprisoned. It happens every day.

When I give up my belief, several good things can happen: I

will feel less miserable, I can think more clearly and sensibly about the treatment program, and I can benefit more easily from the parts of the program that are helpful. Even though I won't believe many ideas they want me to believe, I can tolerate the system. After I complete my sentence, my appropriate emotions and rational thinking will allow me to be more effective if I choose to inform people about the injustice done to me and to work to change the laws.

If I keep my Belief, I will remain angry, and I may get depressed by thinking that it's too difficult to deal with a treatment that doesn't make sense to me. Also, I may act inappropriately and prolong my treatment. Finally, I may have lasting anger and resentment toward the people who created this injustice, and that will only hurt me.

DIBs for LFT Related to Anger

Low Frustration Tolerance (LFT) sometimes plays a role in creating anger. For instance, you may become angry with others because you have LFT and because you believe that others must not frustrate you. The following DIBs may help when you find that LFT precedes your anger:

iB: People must not get in my way and frustrate me. When they do, they're no good.

D: Prove it!

E: I can't prove it to be true! I don't like people frustrating me but I can find no evidence that they must not. They are wrong, but they are never no good. My belief is false because people do get in my way sometimes. If I give up this belief, I will relieve myself of a great deal of stress and I will tolerate people better when I'm frustrated with them. I can have more assurance that I can keep my relationships with others instead of losing them.

DIBs for Low Self-Esteem Related to Anger

Low self-esteem is usually created by irrational Beliefs such as, "I'm no good," and "I'm inferior to others." You may have low self-esteem with anger when you think, "people should not take advantage of poor worthless me," and "you must not make me look bad because that makes me worthless, and I'll have to get even to regain my feelings of worth." Now, let's look at a Dispute that can help you when you find that low self-esteem is a part of your anger:

iB: People must not think they are better than me; I can't stand it when they do; when they do they are no damn good, and I have to get even.

D: Is there any evidence my Belief is true?

E: None! First, there is no reason others must not think they are better than me. The universe allows people to think irrationally, and that includes people thinking they are superior to me. When they think they are superior, they are not especially pleasant to be with, and sometimes they are a pain in the butt. Nevertheless, they have a right to be wrong, and they are not damnable for their wrong thinking. Second, I don't have to prove I have equal worth because no one can prove that unequal worth as a human really exists. However, I am automatically worth something to myself because I am alive. For this reason, I will do well to eliminate my feelings of worthlessness. If I stop worrying about what others think, I will think more of seeking happiness for myself with my fallible acquaintances. After all, what most people think of me isn't that important, especially when they think they are better than me.

DIBs for High Self-Esteem Related to Anger

As Dr. Ellis frequently points out, anger usually includes high self-esteem or feelings of grandiosity. When you make yourself angry, you may believe that you are a better person than others and that you are not alone: there are other superior people like you in the universe who agree with you and who just can't wait to rally to support you in your condemnation of others. If not, why would you believe it is correct for you to make yourself angry at some people, to damn them, and to insist that they change their behavior? Also, feelings of grandiosity and superiority, such as, "I am great and certainly better than you," create a "good" feeling along with anger. This is one reason people do not want to give it up—they like to feel good. Here is a DIBs that can help you when your anger includes high self-esteem or grandiosity:

iB: I am better than you, and there are other superior people who think like me. Therefore I have a right and even obligation to demand that you change yourself to please me and to please others like me.

D: Is there any evidence that my Belief is true?

E: No! This is nonsense! I can do some things better than others—I may be more intelligent, talented, and achieving—but that doesn't make me superior to others, nor does it give me the right to insist that they change. Besides, I can defeat myself with my demands because other people can easily notice that I am disturbed, and they may quickly dismiss my opinions by correctly thinking that I am just another screwball. I will do better to accept that other people are fallible, and use my talents and intelligence merely to state my opinions without thinking that other people are inferior and without insisting that they change.

Work at Accepting Human Fallibility and at Only Being Annoyed

As you work to eliminate your anger, it's good to realize that all humans are fallible and, therefore, they make mistakes. With this rational Belief about people, you can accept others, as well as yourself, knowing that people create both bad and good behaviors. As stated before, you can work to change what you can, accept what you can't change, and then move on.

Unfortunately, some people can be extremely ignorant, disturbed, or selfishly uncaring of others. So, when these people act badly toward you, they are usually not purposefully trying to harm you. When you see how pathetically disturbed they are, it would be more appropriate for you to feel sad about their mistakes rather than to feel angry. Accept that it's bad when they don't act as you want, but not awful.

Most likely, when you eliminate your anger, you still will not like everyone; liking people isn't the first outcome of eliminating anger—annoyance is. Annoyance, remember, is not a weaker form of anger—it is an appropriate emotion for disliking behavior without the absolutistic *must*. You can have zero anger while being 99% annoyed. With annoyance, you only have strong preferences. So if someone treats you badly, feel your annoyance and try to change what you don't like. Then work to accept what you can't change.

In REBT, we do not expect or encourage you to like the bad behavior of others or to like those people who continually act inappropriately. Acceptance is what we aim for. Acceptance is simply acknowledging the bad event without disturbing yourself. It is telling yourself, "I don't like it, but that's the way it is." After you have tried to change the situation and failed, you may think, "Now that I am not going to beat my head against the wall about that, how can I go about doing something more productive?"

With acceptance, you have greater freedom to distinguish between whether your attempts to change things will succeed or whether you will do better to move on. With acceptance, you can also forgive others and tolerate their imperfections. When tolerating others, you can interact and associate with a wider variety of people to your benefit and happiness. However, it is important to understand that acceptance is not indifference. Indifference is thinking, "It doesn't matter." When people act badly, it does matter! So it is more beneficial for you to be helpfully annoyed and tolerant than indifferent or angry.

So how can annoyance help you more than anger? With annoyance, you can feel bad—not miserable—and you can recognize that you do care and that the actions of others do matter. But you don't overly focus on the bad actions of others. Then you can accept their fallible nature and even work at helping them change if possible. You can continue to feel appropriately annoyed at the bad behavior of others and, at the same time, retain your ability to relate effectively to them. Then you can live and work more happily, interacting in an acceptable and mutually satisfying manner with your fallible family, friends, and associates.

Rational Self-Statements

Rational Self-Statements may help you manage difficult situations effectively. Of course, many events at which you anger yourself occur without warning, so managing your anger well requires practice. Disputing is usually the best technique. After Disputing your irrational Beliefs, work on Rational Self-Statements such as the following:

Others are fallible human beings who will sometimes interfere with my happiness. I can accept that and refuse to upset myself.

I want others to treat me nicely, but they do not have to.

I do not like being treated badly, but I can stand it.

I can tolerate people who act badly.

I do not have to spend so much time thinking of the bad acts of others.

A Summary of Steps for Eliminating Anger

First, think of the bad behaviors or bad actions of a person or organization which you believe should not have occurred— behaviors or actions that you believe interfere with your happiness or act against your values. Then go through the following steps to eliminate your anger. And remember—it is anger that *you* created:

- Recognize bad behavior or events that you dislike.

- Consider how badly you behave when you are angered and enraged, and think of the bad consequences of your behavior, both to yourself and to others.

- Think of the good that you can make happen if you act annoyed rather than angry.

- Discover your irrational Beliefs by doing the ABCs.

- Use DIBs to Dispute your irrational Beliefs including *shoulds, can't stands, awfuls, all-or-nothing thinking,* and *thoughts of damnation and punishment.*

- Develop some Rational Self-Statements and repeat them many times.

- Work to eliminate thinking excessively about the bad acts of other persons or organizations.

- Develop respect, understanding, and tolerance for others.

- Take action according to your rational Beliefs—not your irrational ones.

- Try to help other persons change if possible (or effect change in organizations).

- Work on this 20 to 30 minutes a day for a month.

Conclusion

It is irrational to overly focus on the bad behavior of others and to make yourself judge, jury, and hangman, especially when you consider that your purpose on this planet is to survive and to enjoy yourself. There is no reason that people must change their behavior to please you, and when they do not, you can stand it. Upsetting yourself can easily sabotage your ability to live and work happily with others. Anger can lead to arguments and fights and can contribute to the disruption of your relationships with others. When you are upset with a behavior or situation, identify the irrational thinking that creates your angry feelings and eliminate it by Disputing. Then develop your rational thinking and behavior to manage these difficulties. Finally, try to effect a rational and constructive solution. When you have done what you can and things do not work out, move on and refuse to dwell on the problem. Instead, focus on your goals for attaining happiness!

16

How to Tolerate Frustration and Start Living

Frustration is a part of living. We may not like it, but it comes with being alive. Events and situations occur that we don't like—at home, at work, and in our society. The old saying, to err is human, is so true. We humans often fall short of even our own expectations. We may want to change, but it's not easy. Just try to change a bad habit—it's hard.

The main source of frustration is dealing with problems and difficulties in the external world—especially the hassles of daily living. This is why accepting frustration and managing it may be the greatest achievement you can attain on the rational "road less traveled" from being abstinent to being happy.

What exactly is frustration? It is failing to reach your goals or having your efforts blocked. Being frustrated is simply the event of getting what you don't want. Feeling frustrated is an appropriate emotion you have when you think something like, "I am not getting what I want, and I don't like that." You create LFT, a hindering emotion, when you believe, "I must get what I want— I can't stand frustration." Like most other irrational Beliefs, LFT begins with absolutistic and unconditional thinking.

How You Defeat Yourself with LFT

With LFT, you upset yourself about your frustration—which easily sabotages your attempts to deal with the frustrating situation. The following is a list of ways you can hinder yourself with LFT:

Exaggerating Difficulties: You can tell yourself, "It's too hard," so you make a mountain out of a molehill by making things seem more difficult than they actually are.

All-or-Nothing Thinking: You tend to see matters as either totally easy or totally hard. For example, you may believe everything for you is difficult while everyone else has it easy.

Dwelling on Difficulties: You may overly focus on the difficulties and frustrations of attaining happiness. Difficulties are real and being aware of them is good. But, with LFT, you think of them far more than is helpful.

Neglecting Happiness: You may neglect to think about happiness. While overly focusing on frustration and misery, you may not think of success, giving yourself little awareness of happiness.

Feeling Depressed: You whine about difficulty and create depression by thinking, "It's too hard to enjoy myself—the world should make it easier."

Feeling Envy: You may envy others when you see them achieving happiness easier than you do. When you believe that others have it easier, you can presume that you deserve better and then whine about how bad you have it. You think that life shouldn't be unfair and, paradoxically, that you should have what others have without working for it.

Developing Poor Self-Discipline: You can find it difficult to work persistently at achieving long-term goals, improving your talents and skills, changing your self-defeating behavior, or eliminating your upsets.

Diverting Yourself Into Short-Term Pleasures: You can easily divert yourself from your important long-term interests by doing easy, short-term activities. These activities, such as watching TV, raiding the refrigerator, or going shopping, can provide immediate pleasure. But they will give you little lasting satisfaction in comparison with achieving your long-term goals, such as developing a skill, getting a better job, developing a satisfying marriage, writing a book, or painting a masterpiece.

Procrastinating, Avoiding, and Withdrawing: You can easily put off doing what you want, avoid uncomfortable situations, and withdraw from activities requiring even minimal effort. You may eventually decline to participate in any activity except drinking. If you remain sober, you may associate with people who have quit drinking, but who are taking very little active part in managing their problems and attaining happiness.

Using DIBs to Eliminate LFT

Frustrations are not a good reason to avoid or to escape. In REBT, we believe that you will accomplish more when you face your frustrations, reduce your upsets, and patiently work toward your goals. You can overcome LFT by developing an appreciation of frustration, eliminating irrational thinking, and pushing yourself when things get hard. The following example DIBs can help when you discover that you have LFT.

iB (irrational Belief): I must get what I want immediately; I cannot stand to wait because waiting is awful!

D (Dispute): Is there any evidence that my Belief is true?

E (Effective New Belief): No! I may want what I want immediately, but my desire does not prove that I must have it immediately. Even though I strongly dislike waiting, I cannot prove that I can't stand it, and even though waiting is bad, I cannot prove that it's awful.

D: Is there any evidence that my Belief is false?

E: Yes! If I cannot prove it to be true, then it may be false. If there is a universal law which states that I must get what I want immediately, then I will get it immediately. Yet, often I do not get what I want as quickly and as easily as I want. Finally, when I don't get what I want right away, I do survive.

D: What good can happen, or what good can I make happen, if I give up my Belief?

E: I can appreciate that I can gain happiness, but that it takes more patience and persistence than I have been willing to give. I will find it easier to work more persistently for the things I enjoy, and I will create less depression and more happiness for myself.

D: What bad can happen, or what bad can I make happen, if I keep my Belief?

E: I may remain depressed, and I may be impatient with others and myself. I may find short-term, easy pleasures very tempting, and I may believe that long-term pleasures are hardly worth the effort. Finally, I will enjoy myself much less.

iB: I must not feel uncomfortable—I can't stand it.

D: Is there any evidence that my Belief is true?

E: No! I may not like feeling uncomfortable—but that doesn't equal a must nor does it prove that I cannot stand it. Furthermore, this belief is false because I have felt uncomfortable before, and I have stood it every time. I will do better when I think less about discomfort and more about the results of doing, even when things are hard. When I *do*, I will procrastinate less so I can accomplish more and enjoy myself more. I'll be less depressed. Otherwise, I may never get rid of my depression, and I'll enjoy myself less.

iB: Achieving happiness should be easy and not hard. I can't stand working hard; it's awful.

D: Is there any evidence that my Belief is true?

E: No! I may want happiness to be easy, but that doesn't prove it has to be. Also there is no evidence I can't stand hard work or that it is awful, meaning more than one hundred percent bad. There is some evidence my Belief is false. Nearly everything I do requires some effort, and happiness sometimes requires great effort. This is evident by the fact that when I don't work at getting what I want, I usually don't get it, and people who work hard often seem to be happier than those who moan and groan.

I can do much better when I give up this belief. I can do more because when I work toward my goals I will focus on what I am doing and how I can do it instead of excessively focusing on the difficulties of doing it. If I keep my belief, I may do worse. I may whine about difficulty for a long time, and I may remain pessimistic and depressed, and never accomplish my dreams or ambitions.

iB: It's too hard to deal with frustration.

D: Is there any evidence that my Belief is true?

E: No, there is none. Difficulty does exist, but I have not proven anything to be too difficult. Instead of avoiding frustration, I can manage it better by facing it—even when I tell myself it's too hard.

iB: Because successful living is easier for others than for me, other people should take care of me.

D: Prove it!

E: I can't prove it. The effort that others put forth for their happiness is irrelevant to my happiness. It is inefficient to want others to provide most of my happiness, because I can provide more for myself than they can. And even if I want them to cater to me, there is no reason that they should.

iB: I have failed so much—this proves it's too hard for me to succeed.

D: Where is the evidence?

E: There is none! My failing doesn't mean it's too hard. It merely means it's more difficult than I expected. Other people facing the same amount of difficulty succeed. I will have a better chance of success when I focus on how to accomplish my goals instead of how hard it is.

iB: I don't feel like doing it, and I can't do what I don't feel like doing.

D: Prove it! Where is the evidence?

E: I can't prove it! My feelings, thoughts, and behaviors go together. Therefore, if I begin to think of the benefits of success and then push myself to get started, I can easily think of even more benefits in working and succeeding. This rational thinking will allow me to feel more like working and following through.

Accept Frustration as a Part of Living

Frustration, remember, is failing to reach your goals or having your efforts blocked. Feeling frustrated is thinking, "I do not like not getting what I want." People usually feel frustrated when experiencing difficulties and disappointments. When you accept frustration as a part of living and work to benefit from it instead of using it to create misery for yourself, you will achieve more of your goals with fewer hassles. To accept frustration, consider the following points:

Difficulty is a Daily Occurrence: Every move you make takes effort, no matter how small it is. When you think "it's too hard," you exaggerate the difficulty; and then you may quickly give up, eliminating any chance of success. Severely depressed people do this. Some don't even get out of bed in the morning because they think the ordinary tasks of living are too hard. Yet, others consider daily difficulties a matter of fact—without considering them to be a hassle. Again, saying "it's too hard" gives you an inaccurate sense of the effort required and, in fact, it may take much less effort than you think. You won't know until you eliminate your LFT and start trying.

Frustration Occurs Quickly and Easily—Happiness Occurs Over Time and Takes Work: Why is it easy to become frustrated? Because, wanting without having can occur quickly, easily, and almost effortlessly, and wanting doesn't equal having. For example, you may see an attractive person and want to be with that person almost instantly. Usually, however, you cannot immediately have the relationship that you want, and that is frustrating. Eventually, you may fulfill your desires, but what does it take? It takes effort—over a period of time.

In any endeavor, to get what you want you first gain the cooperation of the universe (people, other living creatures, nature, and your own human nature). But the universe does not respond to mere wishes. You can want many things—you can wish that others would act better or that you would not fail, or that the world would make happiness easier to achieve. Yet, wanting and wishing aren't enough to make it happen.

However, the minute you begin working, things begin to happen—you get results! At first, the results may not please you, but they are different from what you obtained through mere wants and wishes. After your initial efforts, you can look at what you've achieved, and you can continue to make further gains by altering your approach and by noticing the results, as well as by continuing until you accomplish your goals.

To go from wanting to having what you want usually takes work, high frustration tolerance, flexibility, and persistence. Now, let's go back to that attractive person you want to meet. Let's say that handsome or lovely person develops an interest in you. You will have to discipline yourself to develop a relationship. To do this you can do several things. You can spend time with him, realizing that you may be rejected. You can think about what he likes and work to please him; and you can enjoy yourself with him and adjust to your mistakes when you make them.

What if you hold to the irrational Beliefs, "I must have what I want quickly and easily; it shouldn't take work to get acquainted because I can't stand to discipline myself"? Will those thoughts help you? Not much! The universe just isn't set up to give you what you want when you want it merely because you want it. What will help you are rational Beliefs that allow you to follow through with your desires, Beliefs such as, "I would like to have what I want quickly and easily, but it doesn't happen that way most of the time. So, I will work diligently, persistently, and patiently until I achieve my goals. Even though I prefer an easier way, I can stand it." With this rational thinking, you are more apt to follow through with less discomfort, moving more persistently from mere wants to desired results.

Another reason to accept frustration as a part of living is because it is easier to dislike something than to change it. Let's say, hypothetically, it's Saturday morning and your children are watching their favorite Saturday morning TV shows. You just woke up and you want to sit in your favorite chair (which is in the same room as the TV) so you can read your newspaper. You also have a few chores to be done before noon, and you need your spouse's help, but your spouse wants to sleep in.

It is easy to dislike such things. But just how likely is it that you can get your family to change their behaviors and act as you want? It will take effort which may prove futile. Even though change for them would be better for you, people often think of their desires and not yours, and they may not change for you. If you believe, "My children must remain quiet and make no noise when I am reading, and they must not create problems for me; my spouse is always disappointing me by sleeping in on Saturday; and I can't stand all this," will you then be able to appropriately communicate to your family? Hardly! Instead, you will just add misery to frustration, exaggerate matters, and manage the situation poorly. On the other hand, if you do not make yourself upset, you can appropriately try to change their action. If you are not successful, you can accept it and make your own adjustments.

Feeling Frustration Can Motivate You: Feeling frustrated can help you. If you don't feel bad when you do badly, will you correct your mistake? Probably not. If you don't feel irritated with people when you dislike their behavior, will you try to help them to change? Probably not. And, if you don't feel bad about the wrongs in the world, will you work for change? Again, most likely, no! It's difficult to imagine adjusting to or fixing problems without first having a feeling of frustration.

What if you tell yourself, "I must never feel frustrated; I can't stand it"? Can you then work to eliminate problems? Not very well! Instead, you may exaggerate the discomfort, make yourself depressed, and avoid your problems altogether.

Remember, it is not feeling frustrated that creates misery at not getting what you want; it is LFT. With LFT, you can bog yourself down in a state of depression, or you can impulsively try to avoid or escape your problems instead of facing them. You may think, "The world should make it easier to attain happiness; it's an awful, rotten world that would make it so hard to get happiness; because I can't stand difficulty, I have to avoid all difficult problems." This thinking can give you more problems than the frustration itself. Frustration alone contains no misery, and it can help you do more. With it, you may quickly think, "I am not getting what I want and I don't like that. Because I prefer happiness to frustration, how can I attain it even when it is difficult?"

Take Action: Change Your Behavior!

Understanding your frustrations and Disputing your irrational Beliefs about frustration will go a long way in helping to change your thinking so that you can accept the world as it is. However, in REBT, we do not think that this is enough to enable you to successfully eliminate your disturbances and to live happily. Those things take place when you change your behavior. It is through your actions that you acquire more of what you want. When you act differently, the world responds differently. And when you think more sensibly, you can act more effectively. By eliminating LFT, you can remove it as a hindrance, as well as increase your ability to manage everyday problems and hassles. Here are three common behavioral problems created by LFT along with suggestions on how to change these behaviors. They are procrastination, upsets with other people, and upsets at day-to-day hassles.

Procrastination: Procrastination is the act of not doing, without good reason, what you have already decided to do. To stop procrastinating, pick an activity or responsibility that you have been putting off, such as cleaning your house or apartment, asking an attractive person for a date, or looking for a better job. Next, Dispute the irrational Beliefs that lead you to procrastinate:

Prove that I shouldn't have to do it!

Prove that it should be easier before I can do it.

Where is the evidence that it's too hard?

Prove that I can't stand doing it.

Think of the happiness that you can have when you succeed. Replace the thoughts of difficulty and misery with pleasant thoughts of success. Then, push yourself—get started!

Do what you have always wanted to do—as soon as possible! Even if it's difficult, you can still do it! Again—think how pleased you will feel if you succeed.

Upsets with Other People: Take action to change your behavior when you're overly frustrated with other people. Change your thinking, then take action. Here is an example:

Think of a person who frequently thwarts you. Maybe you know someone who is nearly always late, or who often interrupts when you are talking, or who frequently makes a commitment and doesn't keep it. Now Dispute the irrational thinking that creates your LFT about this person:

Prove that this person must not frustrate you.

Where is the evidence that you can't stand this person's behavior?

Where is the evidence that dealing with that person is awful?

Next, do a Rational-Emotive Imagery exercise by imagining that person acting in a manner that interferes with your expectations and happiness. As you imagine the event, allow yourself to become upset. Hold that feeling for a minute or two, then change your upset to merely feeling frustrated and unhappy. Do this two or three times before you quit and follow through by doing this imagery exercise every day for at least three weeks. By doing this you may soon notice a distinct difference in your emotions and in your ability to react rationally to that person.

Also, act differently with that person the next time you become frustrated with her behavior. You can inform her of your problem with her if you think it will help. This would be wise to do if you have never before attempted to do so when you are thinking rationally, i.e., after DIBs and Rational-Emotive Imagery. Whatever you try, if you are not upset, you will not rant and rave, and you can communicate more effectively. If the person does not change, or if you do not choose to communicate your discontent, you can merely accept the bad behavior and focus on the good things you enjoy with that person. Then you will have both the good and the bad without exaggerating the bad.

Upsets At Day-to-Day Hassles: To help with hassles that you regularly experience, you can work at tolerating common difficulties and frustrations such as rush-hour traffic, long lines in the grocery store, and household chores. Dispute your irrational thinking to eliminate your upsets so that you can deal with the problems that can be changed and accept what you can't change. Begin with a DIBs for eliminating your irrational thinking about daily hassles:

Where is the evidence that I can't stand these hassles?

Where is the evidence that it's awful to get frustrated?

Prove that the world is always frustrating and that it never has anything good to offer.

It makes good sense to eliminate the continual hassles that hinder your daily enjoyment. Once you are thinking more rationally about your daily hassles, you can more easily begin to work to change them. In REBT, we not only recommend that you change your thinking, we also recommend that you attempt to change the events you dislike. After you have accepted that hassles exist and probably always will, you can work to change the things you can change. For example, you can work at doing small everyday tasks quickly and efficiently. You can organize to take fewer steps and to do household chores before they pile up, and you can do preventive maintenance—in the house, in the yard, and on your automobile.

You can also work to resolve the day-to-day hassles caused by major problems. Joe, a member of the Orlando S.M.A.R.T. Recovery group provides a good illustration. His driver's license had been revoked, so he couldn't drive his automobile. He dealt quickly with the hassle of losing his transportation. He first got a bus schedule and located the nearest bus stop. Then, he rode the bus every day both to and from work. He also called the cab company to find out rates so that he could budget his money for the times when he wanted special transportation; and he called two of his friends, explained his situation, and asked if they could help out in the event of an emergency.

After trying this arrangement for awhile, he decided that even these hassles were more than he wanted to deal with, so he decided to move. He found an apartment in a location within walking distance from work with better transportation and more services available. Once there, he only had to rely on his friends for transportation occasionally. Even though it was a big hassle to move, his problem of finding daily transportation was important enough to eliminate by moving closer to work.

Conclusion

What do you get when you eliminate your Low Frustration Tolerance? More fun, fewer hassles, and less depression! And you can work to handle the daily hassles of life, eliminating those that you can and effectively managing those that remain. Then, you can enjoy yourself more with other people because you can accept the fact that humans are fallible and will continue to make mistakes that thwart you. You can also focus on long-term interests, stop procrastinating, and start doing.

17

Yes! You Can Attain Happiness!

You can attain happiness through work and change. It's what you wanted when you started drinking or using, and if you continue to drink or use, you do so because you're trying to find something better than what you have right now. Because alcohol and other drugs don't give you what you want in the long run, you may consider quitting. That can be the beginning of another form of happiness—one that won't let you down so certainly.

What is happiness? It's getting what you want and enjoying yourself. It can be a momentary feeling of bliss or it can be a life-long devotion to a highly prized goal. A part of happiness is managing your difficulties by resolving them or by accepting them. To gain happiness, you're wise to establish a sensible set of ideas to help you achieve your goals. In this chapter, we present our views on happiness and how you can develop an approach to gaining it for yourself.

Why Seek Happiness?

Often people do not appreciate happiness. Some people believe it's not a worthy goal and that no one deserves it. Some go further and teach that humans exist for the purpose of suffering. In REBT, however, we believe, for a number of very good reasons, that it is wise to have an interest in happiness and even a passion for it.

People want happiness, and this desire is second only to the basic desire for survival. Happiness feels good and people like to feel good. When you feel satisfied with your lifestyle, people enjoy being with you more than if you're unsatisfied; and thus it also helps them. Finally, when people seek and attain happiness, they often reduce their emotional disturbances and more easily handle the problems of living.

Seeking and Attaining Happiness

Happiness is getting what you want; it is enjoying yourself and thinking, "I like that." It can occur through choosing to effect good results whenever possible. For instance, it can arise through eliminating a problem and thinking, "It sure is good to get rid of that problem." You may also gain happiness through purposeful activity that includes working towards a specific goal.

When events or circumstances are bad, the best immediate happiness can be gained by eliminating the immediate problems. Then, with fewer hassles, you can seek a different form of satisfaction.

To attain happiness, move toward developing realistic Beliefs about how to attain it. The following suggestions can help point you in the right direction:

Seek Pleasure, Not Merely the Absence of Pain: In working for happiness, it's helpful to apply this principle: seek pleasure beyond the elimination of problems. Happiness involves both attaining pleasure and eliminating difficulties. You may find yourself motivated to act primarily when you are faced with a problem. Then, when the problem is resolved, you simply stop working. It's better to start working for pleasures. Think about it. When you seek pleasure, you think a great deal about it—thereby experiencing even more happiness. On the other hand, when you mainly seek to eliminate hassles, you think a lot about them and experience more frustrations. Therefore, thinking of pleasures is usually better.

You can apply this principle to any important facet of life. For instance, when you seek a mate, you can focus on the pleasures of dating more than the disappointments of rejection and loss. In finding a mate, you can choose one who pleases you instead of settling for someone mainly to eliminate your loneliness. When you look for a job, seek one that you like instead of one that just provides an income.

Seek Long-term Goals: In REBT, we believe you will attain more happiness by working toward long-term goals. With long-term happiness, you concentrate more on your source of happiness; you have more reason to remain healthy because you have greater motivation; and, you can find enjoyment even in the planning. With long-term pleasure-seeking, you look forward to good things in the future and you have fond memories of the past.

In attaining happiness, think about your long-term goals. Many people don't. When I ask my clients if they want happiness, they quickly reply, "Yes, of course." But when I ask them "How much time do you spend thinking about long-term happiness," they frequently say, "Very little." It doesn't make sense, does it? How can you attain happiness if you don't think about it? So, take the time to determine what your long-term goals are, then focus on how to attain them.

Most people achieve long-term happiness by pursuing their interests, for instance, in mating, relationships with family and friends, and in work and hobbies. Some pursue humanitarian interests; others thrive on excitement and adventure; still others develop creative interests. You can cultivate your ability to interact and socialize, or you can practice more solitary activities, such as art or writing. No matter what your endeavors, you can find happiness by pursuing activities that you enjoy. (For an excellent list of activities, avocations, and hobbies, see the appendix entitled "Suggestions For Enjoyable Pursuits" in the book *A Guide to Personal Happiness*, by Drs. Albert Ellis and Irving Becker.)

Discover Happiness: We humans have no happiness-attaining instinct to guide us. We learn through exploration and discovery. Some people find happiness in childhood or in adolescence, and they continue to pursue the interests they developed then. If you weren't so lucky, you can now pursue a variety of activities until you find what's pleasing and enjoyable to you. For instance, if you do not have a hobby or life pursuit, you can try out several activities that you think you might enjoy.

Take Risks: Most people who find happiness take risks. In our view, taking risks usually means taking action in situations where you put your ego on the line. These are situations where you think, "If I fail, I'm no good," or "I may be rejected and that would be awful."

If you want to ask someone for a date but worry about rejection—go ahead and do it! You risk failure, but so what! The world will not come to an end if the person declines, and if the person says "yes" you will have a chance to enjoy yourself on at least one date—or maybe even for the rest of your life.

When you don't take action, you have a greater risk of failing to attain happiness—in the short run and in the long run! The same holds true for other facets of life. If you have been accepted for a job interview and don't go because you think you will be rejected, will you get the job? Most likely no! So go to the interview! This applies to anything you want. You can think, "Oh, woe is me, I just can't take rejection," and you can worry so much about the bad that can happen that you lose a chance for the happiness and pleasure that you seek—and you continue to keep your worries. Remember the saying, "A coward dies a thousand deaths—the brave, but one." If it's something you want to do, go ahead and do it! Don't hesitate.

Develop Trust in What You Think and Feel: Because ways to happiness vary from one individual to another, you might enjoy a particular activity even though others don't like it at all. So when you feel pleased, it's good to fully acknowledge to yourself that you feel pleased.

Sometimes we do activities that we don't want to do. Maybe we want to please a friend or mate, or maybe we want to gain approval from "the masses." Or perhaps we enjoyed the activity when it was new, but we now have little desire for it. Whatever the reason, by directly asking yourself whether or not you like it, you can more easily eliminate those things that you don't enjoy and focus on those that you do. You can ask yourself, "Do I enjoy this because I like it or because someone else approves if I do it?" If the answer is "Yes, I enjoy it," then consider continuing the activity.

Absorb Yourself in Doing What You Like: After you have found an activity that you enjoy, you can ask yourself, "Can I enjoy this for a long time?" If the answer is yes, throw yourself into it. "Vitally absorb yourself," as Albert Ellis says. Do it until you involve yourself so much that it's hard to leave it! For instance, if you want to enjoy yourself more in your job, commit yourself and follow through. If you're unable to make your work an activity of life-long enjoyment, try to find work that will provide such enjoyment, or at least try to find an absorbing side interest, such as writing the great American novel or painting a masterpiece—or playing music, breeding animals, or learning to play chess or bridge.

View Happiness as a Lifelong Endeavor: There's almost no good reason to quit working for happiness. However, there can be exceptions. Some unfortunate people experience severe physical pain to the extent that they believe that they can have no more happiness. This, for them, can be a rational reason to give up, at least until the pain subsides. But, when you experience an extremely bad disappointment or loss—and most of us do in our lifetimes—think of it as an unfortunate event or circumstance, not as the end of happiness! For instance, losing a life-long loved one or friend is bad, but it isn't a reason to never seek happiness again. Accept the fact that it happened, mourn the loss, allow yourself your good memories, and then get on with living. Don't give up on happiness—keep your goals and continue to pursue them. They will serve you well.

Hindrances to Happiness

Even though you may like our idea of long-term happiness, you may not follow through with the work required to attain it. Even when you do, you may encounter obstacles and quit. Let's look at some of these hindrances together with ways of overcoming them:

Inertia: Inertia is the tendency to keep doing what you're accustomed to doing instead of something else. It's one of the simplest reasons people do not actively pursue their desires for happiness. A common example of inertia is that you may find that getting started on a project is more difficult than doing it after you get started.

What does it take to overcome inertia? Effort! There is no way around it. If you want to get started, try the REBT Push-Your-Ass technique! That's right. Do it! Take the first step! Push yourself!

You can never fully overcome the hindrances of inertia because attaining happiness requires starting yourself over and over again. You may as well accept it and start pushing!

Drinking: Heavy drinking (using) and happiness do not go together very well. Drinking and drugging are hindrances because they create so much unhappiness, for you and for people close to you. Yes, they can give you temporary relief from the pressures of living, and, when high, you can forget your troubles. Sooner or later, though, reality comes crashing back down on you.

When you use alcohol or other drugs to escape and to avoid the hassles that occur when seeking happiness, you put drugs directly between you and happiness. So your dependence on alcohol or other drugs is one of the first hindrances to eliminate in attaining happiness.

False Prerequisites for Happiness

Some people have beliefs about themselves and happiness that prevent them from seeking it. Here are two examples:

Seeking Self-Worth Before Happiness: Many people believe that they have to feel good about themselves before attaining happiness. Is this true? Do you have to have a sense of high self-esteem before you can enjoy yourself? Not really. You can think that you are worthless and still feel happy. For instance, you can feel down on yourself , yet, at the same time, you can meet an attractive person and feel pleased, or read a good book and like it, or see a beautiful sunset and enjoy it.

Granted, if you have low self-esteem, you may not enjoy yourself as much and you may not follow through as well in a relationship with that attractive person as you would if you had higher self-esteem. Still, the most direct route to happiness is to push yourself, to try many activities, and to continue doing those that you enjoy. While seeking happiness, you can continue to work to eliminate your irrational Beliefs that create low self-esteem.

Seeking Self-Awareness Before Happiness: Many people seek self-awareness and self-understanding before happiness. Often they ask, "Who am I?" believing that when they find themselves they will automatically know what activities are the right ones for them. Instead of chasing the illusion of "finding yourself," seek knowledge of what you like and how to attain it

Most people who say they have found themselves never lost themselves. Instead, they simply found some form of happiness and they continue to work for it, because of devotion and because they strongly enjoy it. They may not call it happiness—rather, they call it joy, or a reason for living, or the true meaning of life. Whatever they call it, all of these things depict different aspects of happiness, not "finding oneself."

Overcoming Upsets That Block Happiness

Emotional upsets often block happiness. It's easier to become upset over what you care more about than what you care less about. Let's say you strongly want a particular job, and you make yourself anxious about seeking it because you automatically believe you are not worthy enough. You may decide not to apply while thinking, "I can't take the misery of thinking about it; oh well, I will be rejected anyway; it's much easier to avoid this whole situation." The result? You may lose out on a source of great happiness.

The following are other emotional upsets that can sabotage your happiness. When you do the exercises in this book, you can go a long way toward eliminating these blocks.

Low Frustration Tolerance: Low Frustration Tolerance (LFT) prevents happiness more than any other disturbance. Long-term happiness takes work, and people often tell themselves *I can't stand the difficulties* or *it's too hard*. There are enough problems in life without exaggerating them with this kind of thinking.

You have a choice: get rid of your LFT and strive for happiness, or take life easy, attempt to avoid frustrations, and have less happiness. We recommend the first choice. It takes frustration into account—you will have frustration no matter what you do—but this choice leads you to enjoy yourself by doing what you like. The other takes frustration into account and leads you to do little. With it you tend to experience little happiness, get down on yourself for your failures, and whine about life being so miserable and hard. Clearly the best choice is to take your lumps while seeking a satisfying life.

Shame: After you have done something you enjoy, you can quickly sabotage your happiness by thinking, "If others knew I did that, it would be awful." This creates a feeling of shame, which originates from your dire need for approval, and shame can destroy happiness.

In REBT, we believe that you will be wise to appreciate what pleases you, fully admit to yourself that you like it, and then decide whether or not to continue with it, based on a realistic appraisal of the consequences. Of course, be aware that if you engage in some behaviors, people may take actions against you. For instance, you want to have an affair, your mate may strongly disapprove and leave you. If you do something against the law, the legal system and those who influence it may not approve and may even imprison you. In these instances, you may attain less happiness overall by doing what you like.

Shame is a different matter. With shame, you do not realistically consider that the worst consequences may be harmless. Instead, you upset yourself with the thoughts that someone else disapproves and you are worthless, and you quickly give up on an activity that you may truly enjoy. It is wise to eliminate the nonsense thinking that creates your shame. You may then make realistic appraisals of the consequences of your actions and decide for yourself whether or not to pursue what pleases you. This will bring more happiness in the long run.

Perfectionism: After you have succeeded, you may think, "Now that I have done well, I must continue to do well." This Belief can easily make you anxious, thereby interfering with your ability to gain more happiness. Of course, no law in the universe says that you must continue to do well. By eliminating this Belief, you may readily see that the way to attain further happiness is to continue doing what gave you success in the first place. Your *must*, however, prevents you from seeing this and leads you to focus on your presumed worthlessness if you fail.

Self-Damnation: You can diminish or even destroy your recently attained happiness by thinking, "I should have done this well all along. Because I didn't, I'm no good." Of course this is nonsense, but you are human so you might strongly believe it. It creates guilt which easily leads you to overly focus on your presumed horrible failings of the past. That's neither helpful nor fun.

Damning yourself for doing poorly in the past is a lousy thing to do to yourself. If you're doing well now, then focus on how you recently succeeded and then continue. If you think of your past failures, learn from them. Your present successes, when compared to your past failings, truly prove that you failed not because you were rotten, but because you sought happiness in an ineffective manner. Now you are doing better than before. Great! Look to the future and keep going.

Grandiosity or High Self-Esteem: Many people recommend that you work at feeling good about yourself. Their sights for you are set low. You can defeat yourself with Beliefs about your elevated worth. Usually you do better with an inflated ego than one that's deflated. Still, you can do better to accept yourself and to enjoy your successes without elevating yourself.

Grandiosity, though, is difficult to give up because it feels good and because it's easier to attain than happiness. It feels worse, though, than simple happiness. Usually when you think, "I am great," you do not feel as good as when you think, "I am truly pleased." Give up this emotion and the Beliefs that create it!

Helpful Attitudes in Attaining Happiness

We have looked at some ways in which emotional upsets can interfere with your happiness. Next, we will look at different ways in which you may view your relations with others in the process of attaining happiness.

Accept Primary Responsibility for Your Happiness: In REBT, we believe that you can attain more happiness if you work for it yourself instead of depending on others. The following is a list of reasons why:

- You know your enjoyments more than others.

- You are the only one who can seek and discover what makes you happy and then make the decision to pursue it.

- You can refine your skills, talents, and tastes through experiencing different facets of life, thereby attaining far more happiness for yourself than others can possibly provide you.

- You can also create many problems through overly depending on others for your happiness. You may have little respect for yourself because you believe that you are not good enough to take care of yourself. You may demand that others take care of you, then make yourself angry and depressed when they don't. You may have little respect for their rights, thinking they only exist to serve you. And, worse still, if a person you are dependent on leaves you or dies, you may be helpless and unable to take care of yourself.

   At least for the most part, take care of yourself. You'll do better when you are the primary force in seeking and attaining happiness. When you are in the driver's seat, you are more independent and in greater control. Then, you can enjoy others without depending on them for all that you want—and that is good.

Put Your Happiness First and That of Others a Close Second: Why look out for yourself first? Albert Ellis says it best: ". . . that way at least one person in the universe is looking out for you!"

Many people object to this philosophy because they think putting yourself first is "selfish." They define selfish as thinking of oneself while neglecting or ignoring others. However, in REBT, we view looking out for yourself first as a more enlightened, adult self-interest, i.e., taking care of yourself without neglecting and hindering others.

Dr. Ellis once stated, "The highest moral good may be that you take care of yourself." Think about it. If it is morally correct for you to treat others well, then isn't it morally correct for you to treat yourself well?

Put your own happiness first. If you don't, who will? And, who can do it better than you?

Do Care for Others: Long-term happiness involves the approval and cooperation of others. Frequently, when people attain happiness through the use of alcohol or other drugs, they tend to care little for others and even neglect or abuse them. As a result, they often have many problems in their relationships. In contrast, people who seek long-term happiness usually retain stable, relatively positive relationships.

Your friends and associates will be more apt to maintain their relationships with you if you respect them and treat them nicely. On the other hand, if you neglect them, they may abandon you. Worse still, they may upset themselves and try to sabotage you because they are angry with you.

When people are rational, they maintain relationships because they enjoy them and because they share at lease one common interest. If you have entered into a relationship, learn to cooperate. You are contributing to another's happiness and they to yours.

Critically Consider the Advice of Others: The advice of others can sometimes help, especially if you are upset, i.e., thinking irrationally. For instance, let's say that you recently met and fell in love with a wonderful person. However, you're not sure that that person feels the same about you, and you shyly withhold your feelings. You think: "I might be rejected and I must not be rejected—I like this person too much. It's too hard to deal with relationships. I may as well give up—it's better to leave while I'm still ahead."

"You're nuts," a friend tells you. "You're kidding yourself—you care about this person and you'd do better to stick it out!" Your friend seems right, and you'd do well to listen.

Nevertheless, it's critical that you weigh the advice of others against your own experience and judgment. Do not be "automatically" swayed—decide for yourself whether the advice can help or hinder you, and make decisions for yourself.

Accept and Respect the Differences in Others: Sometimes you may upset yourself at others because of differences such as sex, race, culture, and nationality. This is a waste of time. Focus on your goals and do not bother with matters that do not pertain to them.

Happiness and Friends: Friends are usually people who enjoy the same forms of happiness. As you change, your preferences change, and you can lose interest in old forms of happiness. You may even lose interest in your old friends when they stay with activities that once brought you happiness, but now do not. For instance, you may have been a member of an organization and have many buddies in it, but you no longer share the same interests with these old friends. Yet you may not want to leave them. Instead, you may want to shake them and say, "Hey! Look what I've found. Join me! It's so much better than what we've been doing!"

Well, you can try. If it works, and if they join you—good! But if it doesn't work, you may consider leaving them. You can enjoy yourself more if you find friends who share what you now enjoy instead of trying to keep old friends who continue with activities that no longer appeal to you. It may be difficult, but it's a part of life when you change, and you can do it.

Happiness and Your Family: If you become upset with different individuals in your family, it's wise to remember that you value your family, regardless of your upset. So take responsibility for your own upsets—you create them, not your family—and work at eliminating your upsets as well as preventing further ones. Your family is more important to you than your friends, so you will be wise to work harder at not disturbing yourself with them.

Consider these points when working through family difficulties. First, there is no reason that your family must treat you nicely, kindly, or fairly, and there is no reason that they must agree with your opinions and behavior. You may want them to do all of these things, but there is no law in the universe which says they have to. They are never damnable or no good for treating you badly. It is bad when they treat you unkindly or unfairly, but not awful. And you can stand it when they are unkind, unfair, or indifferent.

Second, there is no reason that you must gain the acceptance of family members for your opinions or for your behavior. When you fail to gain their acceptance, it's bad, but not awful. They have their opinions and you have yours, and these are often different.

Finally, there is no reason that family living must be pleasant and easy all of the time. Even though you have chosen to live closely with your family, it is often unpleasant and difficult to do. But it is not so unpleasant or difficult that you can't stand it. Sometimes it may be bad, but it's not awful. And, it's helpful to remind yourself that family living has advantages: you do gain some happiness with your family.

Drinking/Drugs Interfere with Long-Term Happiness

Drinking (drugging) is a form of short-term happiness which gives you temporary relaxation and relief. When you work at long-term happiness without drinking, you have at least one good reason not to depend on alcohol or drugs as your main source of pleasure. Bob is a good example. At age 42, he had used just about every drug on the street, but he took less drugs when they began to interfere with his work. He told me during a therapy session, "I don't like to take drugs as much now because I like my business, and the drugs keep me from doing my work." Several members of the Orlando S.M.A.R.T. Recovery group, have stated the same. They said that once they achieved happiness without alcohol, they stopped wanting to drink and now believe that they would have a lot to lose by returning to alcohol.

What Happiness Means to You

Attaining happiness is a unique, individual pursuit. As mentioned earlier, attaining happiness requires thinking, risk-taking, discovery, and persistent work. This chapter has discussed many aspects of happiness. To help you in this pursuit, try asking yourself the following questions about your own personal happiness. They help you to challenge and to think about your present Beliefs, and to determine if your thinking and behavior are leading you to the happiness you want. Choose any activity that you think might lead to happiness and ask yourself these four questions:

Do I like this activity?

Do I know of any activities that can give me more long-term happiness with fewer problems?

Are there pleasures I've enjoyed more that are better than this one?

Can I look forward to enjoying this activity for a long time?

Rational Self-Statements

In working to attain happiness, you can tell yourself the following Rational Self-Statements to help support your rational thinking, as well as to motivate you in working for your own personal happiness:

Today, nearly every step I take will be to attain happiness.

Seeking happiness for myself may be the highest moral good I can do.

I create most of my happiness.

When I neglect my friends or family today, they may neglect me tomorrow.

It would be nice to have the easy pleasures that alcohol gives me, but I won't drink. I can do better for myself by doing something else.

Conclusion

Happiness is doing what you like and enjoying yourself. In REBT we believe that the best happiness is a long-term venture in which you are vitally absorbed. It is an individual pursuit that requires work. The Beliefs and methods discussed in this chapter can help you attain happiness without the use of alcohol or drugs. By eliminating your irrational thinking, you can gain more freedom to strengthen your new rational Beliefs. We recommend reviewing this chapter often and incorporating these practical ideas into your way of thinking about happiness. Then go for it!

18

Help Yourself with the Help of Others: Join a S.M.A.R.T. Recovery Self-Help Group!

The Scene: A room where a small group has gathered—somewhere in your local area. The coordinator opens the meeting:

"All of us here want to welcome you to S.M.A.R.T. Recovery. Our purpose is to help you to quit drinking or using by helping you change the thinking and behavior that contribute to drinking and using, and by helping you work toward the goal of long-term happiness."

This is the beginning of a typical S.M.A.R.T. Recovery self-help group meeting. SMART meetings provide support and information that can help you help yourself to quit, as well as help in your recovery process. These meetings are the only free, nationally available self-help meetings based on Rational Emotive Behavior Therapy (REBT), the basis of this book.

Across the country, SMART meetings may differ somewhat in how they are run, but the central theme remains the same—a change in thinking is the primary impetus for a change in behavior. Join us now as we continue with the meeting.

Ann, the coordinator, presents a statement on the philosophy of S.M.A.R.T. Recovery, along with an overview of the organization. Next, she asks the people attending to introduce themselves. Some use their first name only; others give their full name.

Now that the introductions are finished, Ann asks the group a few questions:

"When you think of drinking, what troublesome thoughts do you have? What specific emotional upsets of your own do you want to work on and eliminate? Now, who has a problem that they want to work on tonight?"

(Coordinators are usually lay people who have been sober three months or more, but not all have had problems with drinking. S.M.A.R.T. Recovery does not believe that only people who have recovered or who are recovering from an addiction can help those still addicted. We believe, rather, that it is important for coordinators to have a sincere desire and ability to help people. Thus, coordinators come from different backgrounds.)

A member presents his problems to the group. Other members then help by using the ABCs, Disputing, discussion, practical advice, and other REBT techniques. One at a time, individuals join in with their own problems and concerns, and the group works on their problems. After Disputing irrational Beliefs, other group members offer practical advice. The reason for this is that advice is best given after DIBs, because people can listen and understand better when their thinking is more rational.

In the open group discussions, members give advice and share their experience on how the principles of REBT helped them deal with their drinking problems. When you listen to their stories, you can see how REBT can help you, too! Let's listen. They are discussing why they didn't want to give up booze and some of the results of their quitting.

Mary, a member, is speaking. "I used to think I had to drink to be accepted by others and have a good time. Then I found out I can like myself without drinking.

"Yeah, I know what you mean," Joe states. "I thought I was a bore if I didn't drink. But after I quit, I found that I enjoy myself just as much, and I'm doing even better at work."

"I used to think I had to be a tough guy," says Tom. "I'd hang out in bars in the small town I lived in, and I had some pretty bad fights. After I quit, I got into less trouble, and I'm sure I'll live a lot longer."

"Yeah," says Craig. "I didn't want to quit either. But when I quit I found out how nice it was to drive home from a meeting without worrying about seeing a red light flashing in my rear view mirror. I used to worry about that a lot."

Martha begins speaking about what she has learned in the group: "One thing the group helped me with is to pay attention to my thinking. Once I realized that my thinking led me to drink, it was easier to see how I could change. And, after I disputed the idea that life should give me what I want with no hassles, it was easy for me to see how wacky my thinking really was, and I began to do more. I was able to accomplish more, and I got rid of my depression."

"I've got a problem and I want to try some of your techniques," says Carl, a new member. "Tell me how the ABCs work."

Ann, the coordinator, replies: "OK. What's the problem you want to work on?"

Carl: "I keep thinking about drinking. I don't have cravings too much, but sometimes I do and I get worried about, well, what if I go back to drinking?"

Ann: "OK, you're worried. You're feeling tense and anxious aren't you?"

Carl: "Yeah, I guess so."

Ann: "Well, in the ABCs your tension and anxiety is the C, your Consequent emotional reaction."

Carl: "OK."

Ann: "Now, what is the event that you're worrying about?"

Carl: "I'm worried about giving in and having a drink."

Ann:"That's the A in the ABCs, the Acvtivating event. That's what you're thinking about that you're upset about. Right?"

Carl: "Yeah, that's right."

Ann: "OK. We need to get to the B, your Belief. What are you telling yourself about going back to drinking that's creating your tension and anxiety?"

Carl: "Well, I'm thinking I don't want to start again."

Ann: "OK. That will cause concern, won't it? You don't want to go back, but you know it's possible. You are human and you can make that mistake. But when people merely don't want to make a mistake, they don't worry and get tense and anxious over it. What they do is feel concerned, so they plan ways to avoid the mistakes. And they follow through with their plans. It's when they think something else that they worry. Now, what are you thinking that's more than wanting not to drink that's making you worried and anxious?"

Carl: "If I have a drink, I'll be a failure."

Ann: "That's it! That'll make you worried. It's not just wanting to succeed, it's thinking you're a failure if you don't."

Carl: "I see your point."

Ann: "We've done the ABCs to discover your irrational thinking, but that doesn't do help you eliminate it. So we don't stop there. We challenge irrational Beliefs to get rid of them. So Let's dispute your irrational belief.

"Where is the evidence that if you have a drink, you are a failure?"

Carl: "Well, if I fail, that makes me a failure, doesn't it?"

Ann: "I can see that failing shows that you're fallible, but I don't see where it makes you a failure. Let's see what other members of the group think."

Craig: "No, you're not a failure if you fail. We all relapsed many times, and most of us have succeeded. If we had been failures we'd never have quit. But we did."

Mary: "I don't think it makes you a failure. It just doesn't make sense to think that way. Think of all the good things you've done. How can you be a failure if you've done those good things?"

Joe: "I used to think that way too, and it took me quite a while to stop. You only hurt yourself with that kind of thinking."

Carl: "I see what you're saying. So I need to look at this differently."

Ann: "That's right. Stay with it. It will take a while, but keep working at it just as we did here. And we'll do more of this in upcoming meetings."

You've just heard some of the kinds of discussion that often occur in S.M.A.R.T. Recovery meetings. During the meetings, there are several things you can do that will enable you to gain the most from them. First, remember our goal: to help you to help yourself overcome your addiction, cope with urges to drink (use), and to recover from lapses and relapses when they occur. Second, observe how the meeting proceeds and how people receive help and help each other. Third, and most important, get involved: present an important problem so that others can try to help you with it.

S.M.A.R.T. Recovery teaches that you can change yourself through self-exploration, open discussions, and by using the cognitive, emotive, and behavioral techniques developed in REBT and S.M.A.R.T. Recovery, which is quite different than depending on a Higher Power, as AA suggests. After you apply these techniques to both your drinking (or using) problems and other problems in recovery you have a good chance of continuing and succeeding on your own—independent of group meetings! Some people can accomplish this in a year, but many do well to attend for two to three years. After that, S.M.A.R.T. Recovery groups are there for you when you want to attend. In addition, you are invited to continue attending to make further gains for yourself and to help others, or you may start a new group.

Well, the meeting is almost over, and the coordinator is about to make her closing remarks. (*Note*: You may choose not to present a problem at your first meeting, but when you want to receive help from the group, you can present one of your own problems and see what kind of help you get. Don't hesitate—sooner is better! The best way to appreciate the effects of REBT is to try it for yourself!)

And now listen, the coordinator is speaking:

"It's time to close our meeting for tonight. We invite you to come back so we can help you and so you can help others in S.M.A.R.T. Recovery. For those of you who are new here—if you like what you have seen in this meeting and you decide you want to help yourself in S.M.A.R.T. Recovery, we invite you to make a commitment, a pledge, to yourself to work on your problems in our group and to stay with the group for as long as it takes. With this commitment, we can work together—through thick and thin—for as long as you have significant problems with your drinking, and in getting on with your life.

"And it's important to follow through with regular attendance (we recommend one meeting per week—twice if you want to) until you've given yourself a fair chance to learn and to help yourself. If you decide that you can benefit, make a commitment to attend meetings regularly to deal with your problems and upsets. Feel free to discuss your problems with the group. We are here to help you and support you while you change the thinking and behavior that contributes to your drinking or using.

"And *everyone*—don't forget to do your homework! Read your REBT and S.M.A.R.T. Recovery books and do your Disputing to help you think more rationally. Homework can help you put our techniques into action! In S.M.A.R.T. Recovery, we believe that you create your own change through work and practice—mainly homework! You can receive good help in the meetings. However, most of your change will come from following through away from meetings with the information you gained here. (*Note*: Homework includes reading, doing the ABCs, DIBs, the Rational-Emotive Imagery exercises, and singing rational songs (see Appendix C), as well as strengthening your rational thinking through Rational Self-Statements. More importantly, homework means changing your behavior so that you do what you came to learn how to do. To start, you can do self-help exercises or reading for 20 to 30 minutes each day. By following through with your self-designed homework, you maximize the benefits of the work you do in your recovery meetings.)

The coordinator is still speaking, and offers a closing thought: "You can help yourself by helping others. After you have learned about S.M.A.R.T. Recovery and our techniques, you can give help and support to other members. You can listen to their problems and help them focus on recognizing and eliminating their irrational Beliefs. Your opinion is important to the group! Our research shows that when people use REBT to help others, they also help themselves.

"Have a good week, and I look forward to seeing you here again next week!"

After you have attended SMART meetings for awhile and have progressed enough so that meetings are not critical to your sobriety, you can continue attending for occasional self help, as well as to assist others in their recovery. Many people enjoy helping others; that's why coordinators do it, and you might enjoy it too. Attending S.M.A.R.T. Recovery meetings for the purpose of helping others can be a part of what you do to enjoy yourself, and we recommend that you enjoy yourself for the rest of your life!

Also, it's nice to know that once you are a senior member other members can seek you out for information when they have questions. We do not have a sponsor program like AA, but new members may want to talk with you during breaks or after meetings to learn more. This can help them decide whether or not to make a commitment and how to help themselves after they do.

Overcoming Upsets about Attending Meetings

Many people find it difficult to attend recovery meetings at first, and it's common for people to ask, "Do I have to attend S.M.A.R.T. Recovery meetings to quit drinking?" The answer is No! Millions of people have quit drinking without attending meetings. However, many others do not quit until they begin attending meetings. When you have problems with drinking, a lot is at stake—so why pass up a chance to get help that makes quitting easier?

Why would you not attend? Perhaps you think irrationally about it. When you do, you may sabotage your desire to help yourself. The following are common irrational Beliefs people have about attending meetings, together with examples of DIBs. When you find yourself hesitating to go to meetings or when you're upsetting yourself when you do attend, you can do the ABCs to discover your irrational Beliefs and Dispute them. Also, read through the following examples of Disputes. If you find a Belief similar to yours, study the example carefully and then work at Disputing your irrational Belief.

Anxiety, Shame, and Shyness: These can easily hinder you by keeping you from going to meetings or even discussing your problems with anyone. However, if you don't discuss them, you may find it more difficult to help yourself. The following examples of Disputes can help you eliminate these upsets. This first DIBs helps you to work on irrational Beliefs that usually create shame and shyness and that may create anxiety as well:

iB (irrational Belief): Others must not see my defects; if they do, they *must* reject me and that would be awful; I can't stand it if others know of my mistakes.

D (Dispute): Is there any evidence that my Belief is true?

E (Effective New Belief): No! There is none! I can prove that I do not like others seeing my problems, but that doesn't mean that they absolutely must not see them; people *can* reject me, but that doesn't mean that they necessarily *will*. Also, I can prove that sometimes it's bad for others to know my problems, but I can't prove that it's awful or that I can't stand it.

My Belief may be false because no law in the universe says people must not see my faults. In fact, many people do see my faults. In recovery meetings, it is good for people to see my mistakes; then they can help me.

If I give up my Belief, I can feel a lot better about telling people I have problems and I can get help much easier. If I keep my Belief, I'll feel miserable about telling people of my problems, and I'll probably not attend meetings.

The following DIBs help with irrational Beliefs that usually create anxiety as well as shyness.

iB: I must do well and gain everyone's approval, so I must say the right thing; if I don't do well, I'm no good and a failure; it would be awful to make mistakes and be rejected by others.

D: Is there any evidence that my Belief is true?

E: No! I want to do well and gain the approval of the other members, but that doesn't mean I must. Making mistakes may be bad, but hardly awful, and my mistakes do not make me no good or a failure; they only prove that I am fallible. I can recover from nearly all of my mistakes, so I'll do better to quit exaggerating their importance. My belief is obviously false because I have made mistakes in the past and others have rejected me, yet I survived, the world kept turning, and I was able to do OK afterwards.

When I give up my Belief, I'll feel better because I won't feel so anxious. I can think more of how to do well instead of thinking of possible failures or feelings of worthlessness. When I keep my Belief I may remain anxious, worried, and shy; I may feel so badly that I leave the group without receiving help, and I may conclude that I am beyond help because I failed again.

Anger, Defensiveness, Defiance, and Grandiosity: Anger can give you many different problems. For example, you can needlessly develop conflicts with others, or you can overly focus on others' bad behavior. Both will prevent you from accurately understanding other people's points of view and from seeing their good behavior. Also, you can divert your attention from helping yourself. Here are several DIBs for helping you eliminate your anger:

iB: You (members of the group) must treat me nicely and kindly and in just the way I want or else you're no good; I can't stand it when you don't treat me like I want, and it's awful when you do not act as I want.

D: Is there any evidence that my Belief is true?

E: No! I can prove that others have treated me worse than I wanted, but I can't prove that they are bad or damnable. I can also prove that it's bad but not awful when others act badly, and even though I do not like their behavior, I cannot prove that I can't stand it.

My belief is false because other people have treated me worse that I wanted, so it is possible that members of the group might, too. And even though I don't like bad treatment, I have always withstood it.

When I give up my Belief, I won't be overly concerned about how others act. If they act in ways I don't want, I can take it in stride and put it behind me instead of overly reacting to their behavior, and I can focus on matters that are more important to me, such as helping myself.

If I continue my irrational thinking, I could easily preoccupy myself with others and not pay attention to information that could help me. Or, instead of stating my opinion in a constructive way, I could argue in a hostile manner. As a result, I could enjoy myself less, or I could give up on the group and leave before I help myself.

The following Dispute can help if you like AA and get angry when some of the SMART members speak of their bad experiences with Alcoholics Anonymous:

iB: People must not talk badly about AA; it's too unpleasant to listen to people say they don't like AA and it's awful when they state that they don't like an organization that helps others so much.

D: Is there any evidence that my Belief is true?

E: There is none. The universe allows people to criticize whatever and whomever they want. I don't like it, but I can stand it. Actually, it is to my advantage to listen to criticism because I want others to do well, and sometimes it helps them to discuss the problems they had with AA. I feel better and do better with tolerance for them than with anger.

The following DIBs can help in eliminating the combination of anger and self-downing:

iB: When others try to help me, they think that I'm inferior; and that's awful; they must not tell me what to do and make me feel inferior; if they do, they're no good.

D: Is there any evidence that my Belief is true?

E: No! My belief is false because people often give advice merely because they like to help others. When they give advice to me, it doesn't mean that they think less of me. Instead, they recognize that I have a problem, and they want to help. It's that simple.

When I give up my belief, I will feel less angry, less defensive, and rebellious, and I may recognize that they do not make me feel inferior—I do! If others give me sensible advice, I can readily acknowledge it, as well as use it to my benefit. Instead of becoming upset and stubborn, I will feel good knowing that I can listen, appreciate, and learn.

When I keep my Belief, I won't receive nearly as much help because my irrational Belief directly prevents me from accepting help. If I continue to go to meetings, I will probably not continue for very long.

The following DIBs can help eliminate grandiosity, anger, and Low Frustration Tolerance, all of which can interfere with your ability to help others and yourself in S.M.A.R.T. Recovery meetings:

iB: Because I'm such a great person, when I give advice, others must accept what I say without question; it's awful when they do not quickly agree with me; I can't stand it when they question the wisdom of my advice.

D: Is there any evidence that my Belief is true?

E: No! There is no evidence that I am a great person who will be viewed in awe by others to the extent that they will automatically agree with me. I may not like it when they challenge me—I prefer that they accept what I say without giving me hassles—but they have as much right to their own opinions as I have to mine, and I can stand it when they disagree with me.

My Belief is false because people certainly can question and challenge me, and those who automatically surrender to my comments will do better to give up their dependency on authority and to critically listen to what I say.

When I give up my Belief, I can patiently answer their questions when I know the answers, and work at learning the answers when I do not know them; when I keep my Belief, I may lose my patience, blow my cool, and enjoy the group less.

Low Frustration Tolerance, Depression, and Anger: Low Frustration Tolerance (LFT) is a behavioral and emotional upset that does more to create depression, laziness, and procrastination than any other upset. When you find yourself not doing work that you know will help, look for Low Frustration Tolerance. It may be the reason you hesitate. When you find yourself becoming angry at others for suggesting that you work on your problems, look for the LFT which precedes your anger. The combination of LFT and anger can prevent you from helping yourself. Below is a Dispute that can help you eliminate these irrational Beliefs:

iB: Recovery should be fun and easy for me, and I should be able to get better without work, so you (others) must not suggest that I have to work to get better; I can't stand working hard to change myself; work is awful, and you are no damn good for suggesting that I do it.

D: Is there any evidence that my Belief is true?

E: No! There is none at all! I can prove that I prefer recovery to be fun and easy, but I cannot prove that it should be. I want to improve without work, but I cannot prove that I have to be able to; and I can prove I do not like others to suggest that I work, but I can't prove that I can't stand it. It is bad that change takes work—it would be so nice if it didn't—but it's not awful. I don't like to work—it is an effort to do it—but I cannot prove that I can't stand it. I can prove that the members are giving me a hassle by asking me to work, and I definitely don't like it, but I cannot prove that they are damnable for it.

My Belief is obviously false because sometimes REBT isn't fun and the work isn't easy. If the other members act responsibly, they will encourage me to work on my problems because that's the only way I will change for good.

When I give up my Belief, I may feel less upset at doing the work, and I will find it easier to commit myself to working. I may even begin to enjoy doing it, and I will learn a great deal more and profit more by helping myself become less disturbed and more happy. When I keep my Belief, I may remain depressed and angry which will make it more difficult for me to receive help. Then I won't give it an honest try, and I may simply declare that it doesn't work and look for easier ways to change.

Conclusion

Attending a recovery group can help. Even if you've found that one program, for instance AA, is not for you, you can look for other programs, such as S.M.A.R.T. Recovery. The people that you meet and the stories of success you hear can help you see that you can quit, and you may learn how to do it—and you probably will if you work at it. Appendix D contains a list of recovery groups.

19

Consulting a Professional Therapist

When people think of quitting alcohol or drugs, they usually think of going to a recovery group instead of to a psychotherapist. Yet the bottom line of most psychotherapy is attitude and behavior change, the same as in recovery groups. So if you want the individual attention a therapist can give you, by all means seek one out. Look for one who is knowledgeable about chemical dependency and who uses a cognitive therapy if you like the approach used in this book and in S.M.A.R.T. Recovery groups.

Why Seek a Professional Therapist?

If you are experiencing a crisis and handling it poorly, a professional therapist can help you make a quick assessment of your problems and upsets, sort them out, and help you begin to work on them in an orderly fashion. Or you may feel embarrassed or anxious about attending meetings and prefer an individual therapist to work with you. Although, in Rational Emotive Behavior Therapy (REBT), we do not recommend avoiding the discomforts of shame and anxiety, you still may decide to see a therapist prior to attending SMART meetings to help you eliminate the upsets you have about these meetings. Also, for many reasons, people sometimes do not improve, even if they attend meetings. During these times, it may help to work with a trained therapist who can help you recognize what is creating your upsets and who can help you resolve them.

Finally, you may want the best of both worlds: the individual attention of a professional and group meetings. They can complement each other quite well, and you probably can gain more from going to both than to one or the other.

Selecting a professional therapist is a personal choice. In S.M.A.R.T. Recovery, we usually recommend that you choose one who has training in REBT or Cognitive Therapy because we believe that they are more effective than other approaches, and because we use the REBT approach in our S.M.A.R.T. Recovery groups. (Our advisors usually have been trained either in REBT or Cognitive Therapy; Cognitive Therapy is in many ways similar to REBT.) All in all, it is important to select a therapist who has a sensible approach.

What do you not want in a therapist? First, you would do well to reconsider your selection of a therapist if the one you are seeing insists your problems originate from your childhood and are now in your unconscious and that you must gain insight into those unconscious feelings and events before you change. Second, if your therapist does not work on your substance use or abuse as a primary problem, you may do well to reconsider your choice. In both instances, the therapist is not focusing on your drinking or substance problems directly, and this can hinder instead of help you in the recovery process. Also, you may reconsider if your therapist talks very little to you and merely listens. You may feel better by talking and having someone listen, but we believe information from the therapist is important, and we believe that you will do better with a therapist who talks with you and who encourages you to change your behavior.

Using DIBs to Overcome Your Irrational Beliefs about Therapy

Several irrational Beliefs and unhelpful emotions can hinder you in obtaining help from a professional therapist. Sometimes you may be reluctant to seek a therapist because of feelings of shame. You may think that people will believe that you are weak because you need therapy and that they then *must* reject you. Like most irrational Beliefs, these two are absolutistic and self-defeating. The following are two examples of DIBs that can help you with this type of irrational thinking:

iB (irrational Belief): I must not be so disturbed that I need help from a professional.

D (Dispute): Prove it!

E (Effective New Belief): I can't prove it! There is no evidence that I can become so disturbed that I need therapy, because there is nothing I absolutely must have. Therapy can help, but I don't absolutely need it. There is plenty of evidence that my belief is false; I am human, and humans can become disturbed. I can easily think in a cockeyed way, make myself miserable, and act in a self-defeating manner. I have done this in the past and good advice might have helped me if I had received it then.

When I give up my Belief, many good things can happen. First, I might upset myself less when I think of getting therapy. Second, I can see more clearly whether or not therapy can help me. Third, I can have fewer and less intense shameful feelings when I call a therapist for an appointment. And, finally, I can obtain benefits from therapy. If I keep my Belief, I may avoid therapy altogether.

iB: Others must not know that I am in therapy because they will reject me; they will think that something is terribly wrong with me; that will make me no good, and I can't stand myself when others know of my flaws.

D: Where is the evidence for my Belief?

E: There is no evidence! Some people may reject me, but there is no reason that they must reject me. People can think something is wrong with me, and they may be right. However, nothing can be terrible or awful in my behavior—only bad. In addition, if other people think I have faults, that doesn't make me no good, because my essence is not made up of what others think of me.

There is evidence my Belief is false. I can stand myself when others know of my flaws because their knowing does not force me to detest myself . . . only I can do that. Other people may already know I'm not doing well—they can see that I'm depressed and worried, or that I am procrastinating about resolving my problems. And, finally, instead of thinking badly of me, some people may understand me and give me a break, and still others may even admire me for my courage in facing my problems.

If I give up my Belief, I can think better of myself, I won't be overly concerned about what others think, and I can think more about obtaining the benefits of therapy. Because I will accept myself more fully, even with glaring problems, I may worry less about someone finding out, and I will upset myself less about others knowing my flaws.

If I keep my Belief, I may feel shamed about going to therapy, and I may not go. But, if I do go, I may worry about other people finding out. Then, I may not do as well and continue to feel shame about many other problems as well.

Accept the Fact that You Will Upset Yourself

Once you realize that you are human and that humans can easily upset themselves, it will be easier to accept yourself just as you are—a fallible human being. If you don't, you can easily think such thoughts as, "I must not be disturbed or else I'm weak and no good." Accept the fact that, once in a while, or maybe even frequently, you will upset yourself. And, even though you don't like it, it's a fact you can face. Then you will eliminate your disturbances more effectively.

Donald, a client of mine, provides a good example. He had been a competent technician for many years in a job he enjoyed. He came to counseling for job-related stress—he hated his supervisor so much that he wished she were dead. In counseling he stated, "I feel so ashamed of myself. My parents raised me with better values than this. I know better." Then he asked, "Can I really feel this way—to want her dead?" I replied, "What you tell me is similar to what I've heard from others. People are fallible, and they often become angry with people they don't like. They tend to damn those people, and sometimes they even think of murder. Your thoughts are hardly rare, I'm not surprised."

Should Donald continue to damn himself (his feelings of shame are part of his self-damnation) for his murderous thoughts? No! Damning himself for his thoughts, a Secondary Upset, will upset him even more and easily prevent him from eliminating his anger and his murderous thoughts.

What will happen if he doesn't accept himself? His feelings may intensify: he may damn himself even more, hate his supervisor even more, continue to have stress on the job, and possibly act out violently. However, if he accepts that he is prone to think irrationally, he can then concentrate on eliminating his upsets.

In REBT, we believe that you will do better to acknowledge your fallible nature, which may include severely disturbing thoughts and blundering acts, and still accept yourself. Yes, you can fully accept yourself regardless of the mistakes you have made. With self-acceptance, you can think about your mistakes, work to change them and then continue to seek happiness.

How do you accept yourself when you are disturbing yourself? The best way is to Dispute the irrational Beliefs that create your upsets at your upsets. The following examples are brief Disputes:

Dispute: Where is the evidence that I must not disturb myself?

Answer: Nowhere! Even though I do not like being disturbed, I cannot find proof that I must not upset myself.

Dispute: Prove that I am no good for disturbing myself.

Answer: I can't! A no-good person doesn't exist. So even though I disturb myself, I can't be a no-good person.

Dispute: Prove that I can't stand myself for disturbing myself.

Answer: I can't prove it! I can stand myself because I have been able to stand myself before. I can stand myself now, and I can stand myself in the future.

Dispute: Where is the evidence that it's awful to feel upset?

Answer: Nowhere! Feeling upset is only bad—not awful.

Disputing Your Need for Your Therapist's Approval

Sometimes you may not want to tell your problems to a therapist because you believe she will think that you are no good or worthless. Let's look at two illustrations. Joyce was in counseling. For her third therapy session she arrived in a panic with a diary of her upsetting thoughts. "There!" she said, "when you read this, you'll really think I'm crazy!" Likewise, in one of Donald's therapy sessions, he stated, "I am afraid you'll discover I'm an ugly person—as ugly as I feel inside. If you do, I'll have to believe you, because I need your approval."

When you believe you need approval to feel worthy, you easily try to please your therapist more than help yourself. You may refrain from talking about your problems—especially your worst problems—because you think that you will be rejected, and you may quit therapy without improving much. But you will improve more by focusing on your problems and by attaining help than by working to gain your therapist's approval.

The following is a Dispute regarding your presumed need of your therapist's approval:

iB: I cannot talk to a therapist because he or she would certainly think badly of me and that would be awful.

D: Is there any evidence that my Belief is true?

E: None whatsoever! I can prove that rejection would be bad, but hardly awful. There are good reasons my Belief is false. Other people have lived very well without their therapist's total approval, so maybe I can too. The task for most therapists is to help people like me to get better, and most good therapists can help me—even if they don't like me.

If I give up my Belief, I can do better at telling my therapist about my upsets, and I may do better in therapy. If I keep my Belief, I may concern myself more about my therapist's approval than about my other upsets, so I may hesitate to talk about my problems. Also, I may fail to recognize that some people, especially therapists, often recognize people's problems without condemning the person who has them.

DIBs: Does Therapy Magically Create Upsets?

You may believe that external events or individuals, such as a therapist, create or worsen your emotional disturbances. However, if you dispute this thinking, you can easily see it's irrational to believe that the act of going to therapy has meaning beyond merely seeking help. Look at the following Disputes:

iB: My therapist may discover that I am worthless and that would make me even more worthless.

D: Where is the evidence?

E: There is no evidence! Even if I could be worthless, a therapist thinking this doesn't make it so, nor would it make me worse. Furthermore, there is good evidence that my Belief is false. Other people have seen my lousy behavior and thought I was worthless, and that did not make me worthless. So if my therapist thinks I'm a louse, it is highly unlikely it will make me one.

iB: I must not go to a therapist because that would make me a certified nut.

D: Prove it!

E: I can't prove it! An act such as getting therapy never determines my nature or essence. An act is merely an act—seeking expert help —and that's all.

iB: If I get help from a highly trained therapist, it proves I am nuttier than if I get help from someone having less training.

D: Prove it!

E: I can't! It makes no sense to believe that I'm less disturbed if I can be helped by a therapist with less training. The degree of my disturbance is simply how disturbed I am and is completely independent of the training of the therapist that I see.

iB: Getting help from a guru will get me better faster and deeper.

D: Where is the evidence?

E: Nowhere! A "deeper" and faster change comes mainly from two things: how hard I work and the quality of ideas and procedures with which I work. The information that I receive from my therapist is important, but it is also important that I work hard with the information. So, even if I go to a guru, but don't work hard, I will not get much better.

Conclusion

A professional therapist may help you. If you decide you want individualized attention and think that you can use help in overcoming your upsets, do not let your irrational thinking and feelings of shame prevent you from seeing a therapist. Find one with a sensible approach (preferably one with training in REBT or Cognitive Therapy) to help you resolve the problems that hinder your recovery.

20

Continuing Your Work and Your Gains

Since you first started reading this book, you may have used Rational Emotive Behavior Therapy and S.M.A.R.T. Recovery to quit drinking or to strengthen your desire to remain sober. In doing so, you may have overcome some of your emotional upsets and now believe that you will not relapse. So, when do you reach a point when it is good to quit working on yourself? *YOU DON'T! YOU NEVER DO!*

If you want to continue your present gains and to benefit even more, keep working. Why? Because it's easy to fall back, because you can always find ways to improve, and because you will want happiness when you are 90 as much as you do now. By maintaining a practice of thinking of your goals and of how well you are reaching them, and by challenging the thinking that defeats you, you will have fewer upsets and more happiness.

What to Expect from Continued Work

What can you expect if you work diligently and persistently? First, you will accept difficulties as a part of living. Second, you will work on your upsets more. The results will be that you upset yourself less frequently, and you will get over your upsets more quickly. For instance, you will spend less time ranting and raving when things go wrong. Also, you can more easily forgive yourself and others for mistakes and shortcomings. All of this will give you more time and energy to pursue happiness.

Once you begin working persistently on your upsets, you may discover that you have more upsets than you ever noticed. This may sound grim, but, in reality, it isn't. With the good results you attain with work and practice, you can begin to see that you are doing better overall. You will feel pleased and hopeful with your daily successes in managing your problems and in achieving happiness. With a new attitude about living and enjoying yourself, you will develop a greater desire for further gains. All of this gives you far more benefits and optimism than you had when you were doing less.

At times, you may do so well that you believe you are cured of your irrational thinking. But upsets will occur again. So be prepared when they do, and go to work immediately to eliminate them.

As you continue, you may believe that you have reached the peak of your ability to think rationally. However, after continuing your work, you may improve even more and discover that the peak was an illusion. So keep working.

What happens if you just take life easy and coast? You may remain sober, but you'll hardly come close to your potential for happiness. Instead, you may continually make yourself depressed, anxious, and angry. You may do poorly at handling the problems and hassles the world gives you, and you may even view happiness as a pipe dream—only to be found in a bottle. Face it! If you don't do the work, you won't do as well as if you did.

Suggestions for Continuing Your Work and Practice

How can you continue to work? First, set an appropriate goal for yourself. If you have used this book mainly to help yourself quit drinking or using, you can now change your goal from relapse prevention to any or all of several new ones, such as increased self-acceptance, less misery, better health, and more happiness. Your work toward these goals will not be any more difficult than the work you have already done. And with these new ambitions, your efforts will give you a much more pleasant existence.

After establishing your goals, you can work toward them on a regular basis. You can set aside time each day to think of your goals and to Dispute the irrational Beliefs you find, as well as use any of the other techniques and exercises that apply to the problems you find. It is easier to do this work routinely by setting aside time to do it. But you can also do it anytime! You can incorporate your REBT self-help techniques and rational thinking into your daily activities. For instance, one client of mine said he disputed irrational Beliefs while driving to and from work. When you run into a problem, you can think to yourself, "I do not like this, so I want to focus on it and resolve it right away, not put it off. I will begin right now!"

As you continue, expect many setbacks! Even though you believe this approach is good, many times you will not use it. This is because you are fallible. Accept that fact, and when you do not follow through, push yourself to resume your good work. Often, beginnings are the most difficult parts. Once you start, your task will be easier!

Summary of Recommendations

To continue working, don't forget the recommendations emphasized throughout this book. Here is a brief summary of principles and practices you would do well to continue to apply:

- Completely accept that you are fallible. Your fallibility includes thinking in a manner that greatly hinders you in your individual pursuits and in relating to people with whom you live, work, and associate.

- Intensely focus on eliminating your emotional upsets quickly (as soon as they occur) and regularly (several times a week). Follow this practice to give yourself more freedom from self-defeat and toward happiness.

- Forgive yourself your mistakes. You will make many of them. Practice effective self-help techniques and you will eventually improve your behaviors and your abilities to change. Tolerate others' shortcomings and forgive their mistakes. Keep your friendships even with their problems, because you won't find any that do not have them.

- Accept that you are a creature who thrives on happiness, delight, joy, and love, and work to develop your ability to find and achieve these in as many ways as you can.

- Accept yourself with your mistakes and shortcomings.

- Work and practice, and you will eventually improve your abilities to change.

- If you have attended S.M.A.R.T. Recovery meetings and found them helpful, continue to attend and help yourself and others.

- Continue your Rational-Emotive education through reading REBT books and other materials.

- Work on upsets quickly (as soon as they occur) using DIBs and the other REBT techniques you have learned.

- Work and practice—practice and work!

- Absorb yourself in a long-term interest that brings you happiness.

Conclusion

If you use the techniques of REBT as outlined in this book, you can have a solid foundation for rational thinking. Through work and practice, you can eliminate the self-defeating tendencies that give you problems and that contribute to drinking. Sure, sometimes you will become disgusted and want to throw in the towel. Turn around! You can regain your commitment and rationally work to change the irrational thinking that creates your upsets and then move on to attain your goals.

You can quit drinking, remain sober, and continue working with your sights set on enjoying yourself! By continuing to work at eliminating your upsets, as well as absorbing yourself in a long-term pleasant endeavor, you can change your way of existing and establish a different pattern for living—one that doesn't include drinking or using! You can face your problems with an attitude of self-acceptance and with feelings of determination and hope, and you can find happiness through active involvement in this imperfect world. This is a lifelong process that takes work and commitment. Others have done it and so can you. Try it! Begin now and keep moving toward better living and a happier life!

A

Glossary of Terms

ABCs of REBT. A basic therapeutic technique in Rational Emotive Behavior Therapy (REBT). The A stands for the Activating event. The B stands for Belief, and the C stands for Consequent emotional and behavioral reactions. This technique is used to help people discover their irrational Beliefs.

Appropriate emotion. An emotion that helps people achieve their goals. In REBT, there are both negative and positive appropriate emotions. Examples are concern, sadness, regret, happiness, joy, and love.

Disputing Irrational Beliefs (DIBs). A therapeutic technique used in Rational Emotive Behavior Therapy in which people challenge Beliefs to discover their validity. DIBs is the most frequently used technique in REBT and often follows the ABC technique.

Emotional upset. An emotion usually accompanied by irrational thinking that easily keeps people from achieving their goals. Examples are depression, anxiety, anger, guilt, Low Frustration Tolerance, and grandiosity. The same as emotional disturbance.

Irrational Belief (iB). A Belief that easily defeats people in achieving their goals. The irrational Beliefs most frequently discussed in REBT are those in which people start with a rational Belief and add an absolutistic and unconditional Belief such as *should, ought, must, awful, horrible, terrible*, and *can't stand*. For example, someone has the rational Belief, "I want to stay sober," and then adds a *must* so the Belief becomes "I *must* stay sober." ("Belief" is often capitalized when it appears within a sentence because of its importance in the theory of REBT.)

Rational Belief (rB). A Belief that helps people achieve their goals. The rational Beliefs most often discussed in REBT are those reflecting wants, desires, or preferences. An example is, "I want to succeed at staying sober."

Rational Emotive Behavior Therapy (REBT). A theory of psychotherapy introduced in 1955 by psychologist Albert Ellis. It states that thinking and emotions are practically the same and that changing thinking can greatly assist in changing emotional disturbances and behavioral problems. This theory gave rise to a widely known approach to psychotherapy called Cognitive Behavior Therapy.

Rational Emotive Imagery. A therapeutic exercise in REBT in which people are asked to imagine the event about which they are upset, allow themselves to feel upset, then change the emotional upset to an appropriate emotion. It is often used following Disputing irrational Beliefs (DIBs), but it can be used alone.

Secondary Upset. An upset about an upset. People often notice that they are upset, depressed for instance, and they become upset about being upset. The second upset is called a Secondary Upset, and the first upset is called the Primary Upset. An example is, "I *can't stand* feeling depressed, and I *must not* be disturbed." The Secondary Upset more than doubles individuals' disturbances. In REBT, we recommend that the Secondary Upset be eliminated before the Primary Upset.

B

Recommended Sources of Help

S.M.A.R.T. Recovery
(Self Management And Recovery Training)
24000 Mercantile Road
Beachwood, OH 44122
Phone: (216) 292-0220

SMART is a recovery organization for lay persons. It uses Rational Emotive Behavior Therapy as a significant part of its program. SMART maintains a listing of existing self-help groups, recommended readings, and items that can be ordered through its bookstore. Items currently available from the bookstore include the Primer on S.M.A.R.T. Recovery by William Knaus, Ed.D., the member's manual, and the coordinator's manual, both authored by members of the S.M.A.R.T. Recovery program committee.

Institute for Rational-Emotive Therapy
45 E. 65th St.
New York, NY 10021
Phone: 1 (800) 323-IRET or (212) 535-0822.

The Institute founded by Albert Ellis, Ph.D. IRET maintains a catalogue of books, tapes, and pamphlets that can be ordered, as well as announcements of workshops for professionals and lay people. All materials and workshops are based on Rational Emotive Behavior Therapy.

C

Rational Humorous Songs

The following Rational Humorous Songs can help you with some of your emotional issues. Most have lyrics written by Albert Ellis that refer to or contain irrational thinking. When you sing them, you may find that you laugh at yourself as you become more aware of your irrational Beliefs.

The following song with lyrics by Albert Ellis can help you acknowledge problems with drinking. Sing it and notice how you feel. If you laugh at yourself, good: you can look at your behavior with a sense of humor. However, if you notice yourself becoming upset, recognize that you may be causing yourself problems with your drinking and with other behaviors that you do not fully accept.

Drinking is the Thing for Me
(Tune: Yankee Doodle)

Drinking is the thing for me!
With it's stinking thinking,
I can feel alive and free
When I'm really shrinking!
Drinking, drinking, keep it up!
With the booze be handy!
Keep pretending, yup yup yup,
That I am fine and dandy!

When I'm acting like a fool
And my ways are shitty,

Drinking makes me feel real cool
And immensely witty!
Drinking, drinking, keep it up!
With the booze be handy!
Keep pretending, yup yup yup,
That I am fine and dandy!

*(Copyright © 1977, 1991
Institute for RET)*

Whenever you strongly believe that you *can't stand* frustrations without alcohol and its quick fix, you can sing the following Rational Humorous Song. It can help you lighten up and quit drinking to deal with your problems.

Whine, Whine, Wine!
(To the tune of the *Yale Whiffenpoof Song*, by Guy Scull)

I cannot have all of my wishes filled,
Whine, Whine, Wine!
I cannot have every frustration stilled,
Wine, Wine, Wine!

Life really owes me the things that I miss,
Fate has to grant me eternal bliss!
And if I *must* settle for less than this-
Wine, Wine, Wine!

*(Song lyrics by Albert Ellis, copyright © 1977,
1991 Institute for RET)*

The following Rational Humorous Song may help you with Low Frustration Tolerance, one of the major contributors to addiction, procrastination, impulsive behavior, and depression. And, like to song just above, it can help you recognize and combat the temptation to deal with frustrations by drinking or using.

Life Should Be Easy
(Tune: "Two Little Love Bees"
from *The Spring Maid,* by Heinrich Reinhart)

Life should be easy or I quickly cop-out
When it's rough or sleazy I begin to drop out
When life is hard, I quickly give my all
To pills or drugs or alcohol.

Life should be easy, people should be caring
For if they don't please me, I am most despairing
I cannot stand the slightest bit of strife
For I demand the easy life.

The next song, like the previous one, can help you deal with the tendency to cop out on difficulties by drinking instead of managing the problems.

Drink Drink Drink
(Tune: *The Band Played On,* by Charles B. Ward)

When anything slightly goes wrong with my life
I just drink, drink, drink!
Whenever I'm stricken with chicken shit strife,
I fall off the brink!
When life isn't fated
To be consecrated,
I can't tolerate it at all!
When anything slightly goes wrong I just sink
Into drink, drink, drink!

(New Lyrics by Albert Ellis, copyright © 1977, 1991 Institute for RET)

To help you accept imperfection in yourself and in others, you can sing this Rational Humorous Song.

Perfect Rationality
(Tune: *Funiculi, Funicula,* by Luigi Denza)

Some think the world must have a right direction,
And so do I! And so do I!
Some think that with the slightest imperfection,
They can't get by—and so do I!
For I, I have to prove I'm superhuman,
And better far, than people are!
To show I have miraculous acumen,
And drink ten straight, to show I'm Great!

Perfect, perfect rationality!
Is, of course the
Only thing for me!
How can I ever think of being
If I must live fallibly?
Rationality must be a perfect thing for me!

*(New Lyrics by Albert Ellis, copyright ©
1977, 1991, Institute for RET)*

The following two songs can help when you strongly believe that you *must* have love.

I Love You Unduly
(Tune: *I Love You Truly,* by Carrie Jacobs Bond)

I love you unduly, unduly, dear!
Just like a coolie, I persevere!
When you are lazy and act like a bore,
I am so crazy, I love you more!
I love you truly, truly, dear!
Very unduly and with no cheer!
Though you're unruly and rip up my gut,
I love you truly—for I'm a nut!

I Am Just A Love Slob!
(Tune: *Annie Laurie*, by Lady Scott)

Oh, I am just a love slob,
Who needs to have you say
That you'll be truly for me
Forever and a day!
If you won't guarantee
Forever mine to be,
I shall whine and scream and make life stormy,
And then la-ay me doon and dee!

(New Lyrics by Albert Ellis, copyright © 1977,
1991 Institute for RET)

Sing this song to help yourself overcome procrastination and the tendency to demand that others do for you instead of you doing for yourself.

Maybe I'll Move My Ass
(Tune: *After the Ball*, by Charles K. Harris)

After you make things easy,
And you provide the grass.
After you squeeze and please me,
Maybe I'll move my ass!
Make my life nice and breezy,
And serve me glass by glass!
And, possibly, if things are easy,
I'll move my ass!

(New Lyrics by Albert Ellis, copyright © 1977,
1991 Institute for RET)

Sing the following song containing lyrics by Philip Tate, and you can help yourself with some irrational Beliefs about seeing a therapist.

Battle Hymn of a Reluctant Therapy Client
(Tune: *Battle Hymn of the Republic*)

I have just discovered that I *ought* to see a shrink,
'cause my thinking and my acting may soon push me to the brink.
And I'm squirming as I'm groping for excuses that don't stink,
'cause I *must* never go.

Miracle, please come relieve me.
Grant excuses that appease me.
Do it quick and make it easy
'cause I *must* never go.

Every human in the universe will think that I'm a nut,
If they do, I'm sure they're right, because I feel it in my gut.
So I will gather misery by hiding in a rut,
'cause I *must* never go.
Cannot stand if they poo-poo me
I get low and sort o'loony.
I'll just masquerade and fool thee,
Then I will never go.

Getting into therapy will only go to shore-
Up my deeply held convictions that I'm rotten to the core.
If my therapist should hate me, I'll be happy never more
So I *must* never go.
Someone help me
Won't you please me?
Tell me I'm okay and squeeze me
Boost my ego so I'll easily
Feel good and never go.

(*New Lyrics by Philip Tate, Copyright © 1989
by Philip Tate*)

D

Alcohol/Addictions Self-Help Organizations

The Baccus Society
P.O. Box 100430
Denver, CO 80250-0430
Phone: (303) 871-3068
FAX: (303) 871-2013

*(Baccus is intended to
promote moderation
in alcohol use by
college students)*

Men For Sobriety
P.O. Box 618
Quakertown, PA 18951
Phone: (215) 535-8026

Moderation Management
P.O. Box 6005
Ann Arbor, MI 48016
Phone: (313) 930-6446

*(MM is for those who desire
to moderate their drinking
rather than abstain)*

Rational Recovery
P.O. Box 800
Lotus, CA 95651
Phone: (916) 621-2667
FAX: (916) 621-2667

Secular Organizations for Sobriety
5521 Grosvenor Blvd.
Marina Del Rey, CA 90066
Phone: (310) 821-8430

S.M.A.R.T. Recovery
24000 Mercantile Rd.
Beachwood, OH 44122
Phone: (216) 292-0220
FAX: (216) 831-3776
E-mail: SRMail12@aol.com

Women For Sobriety
P.O. Box 618
Quakertown, PA 18951
Phone: (215) 536-8026

List provided by Vince Fox

Bibliography

Self-Help Books

Ellis, A. (1982). *A guide to personal happiness.* North Hollywood, California: Wilshire Books. An excellent brief presentation of REBT theory. Contains a very useful list of pleasant activities that can help people cultivate happiness. Also contains dialogues between a therapist and clients that help the reader understand why some thinking is irrational. A valuable self-help book.

Ellis, A. (1985). *Anger: how to live with it and without it.* New York: Carol Publishing Group. (Citadel) Helps readers eliminate anger while advising them neither to vent nor to take a passive, non-resistant attitude. It teaches, instead, how people create a *philosophy of anger* and how they may eliminate it, allowing them to live with helpful emotions and greater compatibly with others. This unusually thorough book covers more ground than you might expect from a book on anger and is very useful to people having trouble with this problem.

Ellis, A. (1988) *How to stubbornly refuse to make yourself miserable about anything, yes, anything!* New York: Carol Publishing Group (Lyle Stuart). Ellis' most popular self-help book. It is exceptionally easy to read and is the choice among S.M.A.R.T. Recovery members who are interested in a general REBT self-help book. It is clearly written, down to earth, and practical. Highly recommended.

Ellis, A. (1994). *Reason and emotion in psychotherapy.* New York: Carol Publishing Group (Citadel Press). Ellis' primary book on the theory and practice of Rational Emotive Behavior Therapy. Originally and revolutionary when written in 1962, this new revision presents state-of-the-art information on cognitive-behavior therapy.

Ellis, A. and Harper, R.A. (1975). *A new guide to rational living.* North Hollywood, CA: Wilshire Books. This classic is one of Ellis' earliest and most popular self-help books. It contains excellent discussions of rationality and irrationality, and numerous self-help suggestions. Revised in 1975, it continues to be a standard.

Ellis, A. and Velten, E. (1992). *When AA doesn't work for you: rational steps to quitting alcohol.* New York: Barricade Books. The An important book for recovering people. Presents a comprehensive application of REBT to problems of drinking and quitting, including numerous self-help techniques. It includes discussions of the issues of alcoholism, therapy, and recovery. Clearly written and easy to read.

Horvath, A.T. and Bishop, M. (eds.) (1996). *S.M.A.R.T. Recovery member's manual.* Beechwood, Ohio: S.M.A.R.T. Recovery. A compendium of articles designed to help people quit drinking and begin their recovery using the techniques presented in SMART groups.

Horvath, A.T. and Bishop, M. (eds.) (1996). *S.M.A.R.T. Recovery coordinator's manual.* Beechwood, OH: S.M.A.R.T. Recovery. A compendium of articles on addiction and recovery written mainly to provide S.M.A.R.T. Recovery leaders guidelines for conducting SMART groups. Contains theory and techniques for change along with articles about the S.M.A.R.T. Recovery organization.

Knaus, W. (1979). *Do it now: how to stop procrastinating (revised edition).* New York: John Wiley & Sons. An in-depth look at procrastination. It insightfully describes many causes of and corrective actions for procrastination in a reader-friendly manner. Excellent for people in recovery who're putting off the development of "positive addictions" to replace their self-defeating ones, and who just don't get started on the things that they want to do.

Self-Help Cassette Tapes

Ellis, A. (speaker) (1976). *Conquering low frustration tolerance.* New York: Institute for Rational-Emotive Therapy.

Ellis, A (speaker) (1987). *How to refuse to be angry, vindictive, and unforgiving.* New York: Institute for Rational-Emotive Therapy.

Ellis, A. (speaker) (1978). *I'd like to stop but . . . dealing with addictions.* New York: Institute for Rational-Emotive Therapy

Ellis, A. (speaker) (1978). *How to be happy though human.* New: York: Institute for Rational-Emotive Therapy.

Books On AA and Changes in the Addictions Field

Bufe, C. (1991). *Alcoholics anonymous: cult or cure?* Tucson, Arizona: See Sharp Press. Contains an introduction by Albert Ellis. Presents a brief history of AA along with an analysis of its program. Compares AA and its program with religious cults. For those not familiar with AA beyond its positive reputation, the results may be surprising. Well documented and authoritative.

Fox, V. (1993). *Addiction, change & choice: the new view of alcoholism.* Tucson, Arizona: See Sharp Press. Contains an introduction by Albert Ellis. Takes an objective look at the theories and practices of the traditional approaches to addiction intervention. It evaluates them and lists the forces of change at work in the addictions field. It also emphasizes the need for a diversity of self-help/support programs and outlines the formats and beliefs of nine of them. Well documented, readable, and in tune with modern constructs of mental health. For professionals, educators, and others who desire to understand current trends in the philosophy and treatment of addiction.

Peele, S. (1989). *Diseasing of America.* Lexington, Massachusetts: Lexington Books. A useful and thorough debunking of the belief that some forms of human behavior (such as addiction, gambling, and over eating) are "diseases."

Peele, S. and Brodsky A., with Arnold, M. (1991). *The truth about addiction and recovery: the life process program for outgrowing destructive habits.* New York: Simon & Schuster. Demonstrates that participation in AA or other 12-step groups is not necessary (and generally not even relevant) to recovery from addictions.

Ragge, K. (1992). *More revealed: a critical analysis of Alcoholics Anonymous and the 12 steps.* Henderson, Nevada: Alert Publishing. Contains by far the best description and analysis ever published of the AA indoctrination process, and quite valuable for this reason.

Trimpey, J. (1992, rev. ed.) *The small book: a revolutionary alternative for overcoming alcohol and drug dependence.* Includes introduction by Albert Ellis. New York: Delacorte. (Orig. ed. 1989 by Lotus Press.) This book was written by a former heavy drinker and presents many useful ideas to help people overcome problems with both drinking and AA's doctrines. It formed the early philosophy of Rational Recovery Self-Help Network.

Index

About the Author

Philip Tate was born in Arkansas in 1946. He attained a B.A. degree from the University of Arkansas in 1968. Following graduation, from 1968 to 1972, he served as an officer in the U.S. Air Force. After discharge, he attended graduate school in counseling psychology at Texas Tech University and obtained a Ph.D. in 1977.

He has worked as a staff clinical psychologist with the Veterans Administration Outpatient Clinic in Orlando since 1977, and he serves as an officer of the National Organization of VA Psychologists. In 1986 he began training in Rational Emotive Behavior Therapy with the Institute for Rational Emotive Therapy, where he obtained an Associate Fellowship and Supervisor's Certificate, and where he has worked as a workshop supervisor. Because of his expertise in the use of REBT with addictions, he often receives invitations to speak at workshops for professionals.

Beginning in 1990, Mr. Tate became an advisor to Rational Recovery Self-help Network (RR), and served on its board of directors and executive committee. As well, he edited the RR coordinator's manual, and published several articles in the *Journal of Rational Recovery*. Subsequently, he became active with S.M.A.R.T. Recovery Self-help Network (SMART). He is currently SMART's vice president, a member of its board of directors, and editor of SMART's quarterly newsletter, *News & Views* (all unpaid positions). He has also been active on the local level, serving as an advisor to S.M.A.R.T. Recovery groups in the Orlando area since their inception. He maintains a private practice in clinical psychology in Winter Park, Florida near Orlando.

His hobbies include, hiking, golf, music (listening), movies, and photography. He is unmarried, and regularly visits his family in Arkansas during the holiday season.